Witnessing for Peace

"This book is an instruction manual for peace in the Holy Land. Bishop Younan's witness for peace and justice through nonviolence and interfaith relationships is a flame of hope in the darkness of despair and violence in the Middle East."

—Margaret Payne
Bishop, New England Synod,
Evangelical Lutheran Church in America

"At a time when Palestinians are largely portrayed as violent people, this book, by a 'Palestinian bishop who is a refugee,' is an important corrective and educative source for all those who are concerned about peace among Palestinians and Jews in the State of Israel and beyond."

—H. S. Wilson
Wilhelm Loehe Associate
Professor of World Mission
Wartburg Theological Seminary

"Bishop Younan's book is full of rich surprises. It holds answers that could lead to peace and reconciliation. Most importantly, the book will help the reader understand one of the most difficult conflicts in modern history."

—Said R. Ailabouni
Program Director for Europe and the Middle East
ELCA Division for Global Mission

Witnessing for Peace

In Jerusalem and the World

Munib Younan

Edited by Fred Strickert

Fortress Press
Minneapolis

WITNESSING FOR PEACE
In Jerusalem and the World

Copyright © 2003 Augsburg Fortress. All rights reserved. Except for brief quotations in critical articles or reviews, no part of this book may be reproduced in any manner without prior written permission from the publisher. Write: Permissions, Augsburg Fortress, Box 1209, Minneapolis, MN 55440.

Scripture quotations from the New Revised Standard Version of the Bible are copyright © 1989 by the Division of Christian Education of the National Council of the Churches of Christ in the United States of America and are used by permission.

Cover image: Wall of the Old City of Jerusalem © Nik Wheeler/CORBIS. Used by permission.
Cover design: Ann Delgehausen
Book design: Allan S. Johnson, of Phoenix Type, Inc.
Typesetting: Phoenix Type, Inc., Milan, Minnesota.

Library of Congress Cataloging-in-Publication Data

Younan, Munib
    Witnessing for peace : in Jerusalem and the world / Munib Younan ;
edited by Fred Strickert.
        p.   cm.
    Includes bibliographical references and index.
    ISBN 0-8006-3598-1 (pbk. : alk. paper)
    1. Peace—religious aspects—Christianity.   2. Israel-Arab conflicts.
I. Strickert, Fred   II. Title.
BT736.4.Y68   2003
261.8'73—dc21   2003007219

The paper used in this publication meets the minimum requirements of American National Standard for Information Sciences—Permanence of Paper for Printed Library Materials, ANSI Z329.48-1984.

Manufactured in the U.S.A.

07   06   05   04   03   1   2   3   4   5   6   7   8   9   10

*To all those who commit their lives to the witness of
peace, justice, and reconciliation.*

*In tribute to the memory of my late father, Andria, and
my late father-in-law, Yousef Yakub,
who were refugees
but believed in invincible justice and peace.*

*In tribute to the memory of my late first cousin, George,
who was a victim of the unjust situation.*

*To my church, Evangelical Lutheran Church of Jordan,
which embraced me and provided me with a platform for witness
for just peace and reconciliation, love, and
forgiveness and our partner churches (COCOP),
who give every support that my voice,
the voice of the voiceless,
may be witnessed in our broken world.*

*To my dear mother, Alice,
who continues to uphold me in prayer.*

*To my dear wife, Suad,
for her wonderful love, advice, support, and
partnership in the struggle for witness for peace.*

*To my beloved children,
Anna Liza, Andria, and Martha,
for their absolute belief in a better future of
just peace and security for themselves,
and for the children of our nation and
all the children in the neighboring countries.*

Contents

Prologue

Witness in a Palestinian Setting

I was deep in thought when the sound of gunfire interrupted our meeting at Augusta Victoria Hospital in Jerusalem. It was September 2000, the week for our annual board meeting of the Lutheran World Federation-sponsored hospital. It was also the week that violence erupted in Jerusalem. The peace talks had broken down. Rumors filled every street, whispering that pent-up frustrations over failed solutions might lead many to turn to the gun once again for solutions. Ariel Sharon, a leading Israeli hawk, chose this moment for a provocative visit to the Holy Place in Jerusalem known to Jews as the Temple Mount and to Muslims as the *Haram al-Sharif*. He had been warned. He had been advised not to make this visit. Yet it happened. This was the spark that ignited the second Intifada—the Palestinian uprising, literally a "shaking off" of Israeli rule and domination.

Augusta Victoria Hospital is such a peaceful place. Located away from the hustle and bustle of the Old City, it rests atop the picturesque Mount of Olives. The white limestone complex and its scenic tower are surrounded by the greenery of trees and an oasis of flower gardens. That's why the church decided to build here. Summers in the confines of the Old City were stifling, and families preferred the cool breezes and shaded gardens. So King Wilhelm II of Prussia came to dedicate this structure for the church in honor of his wife, Augusta Victoria. She, too, surely must have remarked, "This is such a peaceful place."

Yet on this September afternoon in the Jubilee year 2000, the peace had been broken by sounds of gunfire. Rat-a-tat-tat. The sounds continued to such a degree that they drowned out our voices in the meeting inside.

"Soldiers," LWF representative Craig Kippels announced. "Israeli soldiers. They're on the fence trying to enter the hospital."

Riots had broken out in the Old City in response to the Sharon provocation. Scores of Palestinians had been shot. Several were dead. The wounded had been brought to Augusta Victoria for care. The families came to gather underneath the trees, to wait, to hope, to pray. Word went out from hospital offices by phone and e-mail to partner churches throughout the world, summoning medical supplies and resources as the number of injuries began to mount.

The gunfire continued. Word now reached us that the soldiers had broken down a door to gain forced entry. Tear gas was affecting patients.

Walking to a window, I observed Palestinians running to and fro seeking cover. Israeli snipers had commandeered the hospital rooftop and were now picking out targets from the mass of humanity outside. Palestinians responded with the only weapons available, the stones from the ground. Violence escalated.

"What shall we do?" I began to ask as I observed this ominous sight. It seemed hopeless. Violence had once again won the day. "What shall we do? More importantly, what shall I do? I, the Lutheran bishop of Jerusalem, what can I do that might make a difference?" I was lost in thought, feeling helpless.

Then the words came to me. "You will be my witnesses." Words from the inner recesses of my mind. Words from school memorization drills as a child. I heard them clearly, as if they were still carried in the breeze by the one who had spoken them two thousand years ago.

"You will be my witnesses." Some think that they were spoken here on our very hospital grounds—the Mount of Olives, where Jesus had led his band of disciples that fortieth day after his resurrection. "You will be my witnesses," he announced to them as they contemplated their role in the postresurrection era. From this vantage point, those first disciples would have looked westward toward the city of Jerusalem and eastward across the Judean wilderness near the Dead Sea. "You will be my witnesses beginning in Jerusalem, in all Judea and Samaria, and to the ends of the earth" (Acts 1:8). Lifting up his nail-scarred hands, the Lord blessed them and called them to be witnesses.

"A witness?" I thought to myself. "How can I think about that at a time like this? How can I think about that when anger is swelling up in my heart? How dare they turn this place of healing into a place of murder and mayhem? How dare the soldiers violate the sanctity and trust of a church-owned hospital? How dare they bring more suffering on these poor innocent people?" Anger has a way of taking over at moments like these. An urge deep inside wanted me to find a big stick and knock each soldier one by one off the fence. I imagined even the possibility of taking revenge.

"You will be my witness," the words of my conscience echoed over the hilltop. A witness of peace. That's the only way Jesus would have done it. "Father forgive them. They don't know what they are doing," he himself said when sharp nails pierced his hands and feet. Nonviolence. That's his overriding message. Love even for enemies. But how do I find a witness of nonviolence when guns are ruling the day?

Outside the window, the blood on the clothes of the wounded cried out with pleas for mercy. "Not now," I thought to myself. "Now is not the time to stand idly by while my people are hurting. 'Turn the other cheek,' you say? They will shoot us in the back."

"A witness. You will be my witness." The persistent voice would not let me alone. Yet passive and pacifist are a long way apart. A witness speaks for justice. A witness speaks for dignity. A witness speaks out for human rights. A witness speaks for a just peace—not only one's own peace and security, but peace for everyone. Like the Old Testament prophets, a witness does not shrink from addressing the political directly. A witness does not shrink from confronting evil directly, and in so doing, one lays oneself open to risk and suffering.

"From Jerusalem to the ends of the earth." It will not be an easy task. "Jerusalem, Jerusalem," Jesus wept over the city. "You who killed the prophets and turned a deaf ear to those who spoke justice and peace." The ends of the earth may be no less accommodating or welcoming. People are tired of hearing about conflict. People want an upbeat message with pleasant words. Yet Jesus did not shrink from the truth. And the cycle continues from Jerusalem to the ends of the earth, and back again to Jerusalem, going on and on. It's the only hope.

"You will be my witness," the voice pronounced this commission yet one final time. The air outside Augusta Victoria Hospital was now thick with smoke and tear gas. A hand reached out to cut through the darkness. Indeed the speaker's hands were lifted up high for all to see. Wounded hands, but victorious hands. His resurrection is a witness of life triumphing over death, of hope over despair. It is a powerful witness. A witness of peace.

Latin Patriarch Michel Sabbah first encouraged me to write about our Christian witness from Jerusalem. "We Christians need to take seriously the theology of *martyria*," he told me. *Martyria*, of course, is the Greek word for that concept of Christian witness. In the Greek text from the Acts of the Apostles 1:8, Jesus commissioned the disciples to be *martyres*—witnesses.

The occasion for that conversation with the Latin patriarch was the papal pilgrimage to Jerusalem in March 2000. The pope's itinerary had brought him to the Dome of the Rock, where Jerusalem's Muslim dignitaries had gathered in a receiving line. Because of my position in the Old City and my long-standing relationship with the Muslim community, I was the sole Christian leader invited to join them. Positioned between Mufti Ikrima Sabri and the late Faisal Husseini, my presence must have puzzled the aged pontiff. He paused in front of me, noting my black frock, the Lutheran *rock*, and my pectoral cross.

"Lutheran?" he asked. His eyes moved up and down the receiving line, and he spoke softly to me, "The rest, are they all Muslims? And you, a Christian?"

I nodded. "I am Munib Younan, the Lutheran bishop. We have a good relationship in this country between Christians and Muslims."

"Good," Pope John Paul responded. He patted me on the back. "Do everything you can to continue this relationship."

At that point, the Muslim leaders went into a room for conversation with the pontiff, and I took this as my cue to take my leave. A Muslim businessman offered to escort me back to Redeemer Church. Our mood was one of elation as we conversed about this successful Christian–Muslim engagement. Perhaps this was to be a sign of better things to come.

Then, as we made our way through *Baba Sinsli*, the gate on the western side of the *Haram al-Sharif*, a voice pierced through our euphoria. "Take off that cross!" We kept walking, almost as if not hearing. Then it came a second time, "Take off that cross!" An elderly Muslim man sitting in the gateway had taken the self-appointed role of guardian for this holy site. One more time he shouted at me, "Take off that cross!"

My pectoral cross is part of my own identity. It defines who I am both as a Christian in general and as a bishop in particular. It symbolizes my calling. It sums up my witness. Like Paul, I carry the mark of Christ's crucifixion on my body. I wear it always, in every place, and in every situation. I do not take it off. How interesting that I had just met with the Muslim leaders of Jerusalem, and it not been a point of contention! They had accepted my cross, just as they had accepted my own presence in their midst. Yet now, I was being challenged by this elderly gentleman who took offense at my cross.

My Muslim escort intervened. "Be quiet," he addressed the older man. "He is our bishop." Then he turned to me, "Don't worry. These extremists don't speak for us."

Nevertheless, this man's words continued to haunt me as we walked in silence into the souk, which connects the Old City with the Jewish Western Wall Plaza.

I was so engrossed in thought that I hardly noticed the Jewish settler woman with her four children. She called out to me and then spat on me several times. "The cross. The cross. The cross," she continued to shout as my escort stepped between us.

Several shopkeepers yelled out, "Pay her back. Pay her back."

I quickly gained my composure and offered a smile. "May God forgive her," I announced. "She doesn't know what she is doing."

Word travels quickly in Jerusalem. My friend Rabbi Ron Kronish telephoned to console me, "We, too, have our extremists. Ignore them."

Later that afternoon when we gathered with Pope John Paul at the Church of the Holy Sepulchre, Patriarch Sabbah reminded me about how Jesus' own witness on the Via Dolorosa and at Golgotha provided the example for Christians to take up the cross and follow. "We Christians need to take seriously the theology of *martyria*," he said to me. His words still ring in my ears today.

Sabbah's words rang in my ears six months later that Jubilee year, when violence broke out in Jerusalem and when our Lord's ancient words spoke out to me from the Mount of Olives. "You will be my witness."

This imagined conversation has passed through my mind on many a day since fighting erupted once again in the Holy Land that September day. From the Mount of Olives, conflict has spread throughout the villages of the West Bank and Gaza, to the settlements and roadsides, to refugee camps and military checkpoints, to the bus stations of Jerusalem and the street corners of Tel Aviv. It has spread to debate-filled chambers of statehouses, to newspaper readers in coffee shops, and to people in church pews across the world. The sounds of the struggle echo from Jerusalem to the ends of the earth.

Nearly a year later on September 11, 2001, I had traveled to the ends of the earth for a speaking engagement in California. While there, I learned of terrorist attacks upon the World Trade Center in New York City and upon the Pentagon in Washington, D.C. I was shocked. I was filled with anger. I was moved to compassion and understanding. Americans were suffering. Americans were struggling. Americans were asking difficult questions. Many turned to me for a word of hope during those dark days. I listened. I condemned the horror and the work of evil. I offered consolation and hope. I shared my witness from my perspective as bishop of Jerusalem. It became obvious to me that our calling to witness had been taken to a new level of importance.

The greater the violence, the greater hunger for a word of peace. Not just a word, a witness. A total life commitment to peace and justice. A witness in word and deed. As I share my story with you, I can think of no more important principle that guides my ministry as bishop of the Evangelical Lutheran Church in Jerusalem, serving churches in Jordan, Palestine, and Israel. Mine is a unique calling, but I do not stand alone. Jerusalem has a long history of Christian witness in a city of diversity and pluralism. My witness encounters Muslim and Jew. It encounters Greek Orthodox, Coptic, Armenian, and a host of faith expressions in an ecumenical setting. It encounters fanatics and religious fundamentalists. Yet the pervading theme is that this witness speaks directly to the situation in Jerusalem, to the struggle of my people for dignity and freedom. I will speak it honestly. I will speak it truthfully.

The message was spoken from the Mount of Olives nearly two millennia ago. "You will be my witness from Jerusalem to the ends of the earth." I can think of no higher calling than to be a witness for peace.

Part 1
Contexts

1

"We Have This Cloud of Witnesses," 1

Two Thousand Years of Christianity in Jerusalem

"So, how long has your family been Christian? When did your ancestors first hear about the gospel? Who brought them the message of salvation?"

Invariably, I am asked by American and European visitors about my Christian origins. People are curious about me in particular and about Palestinian Christians in general.

"It was likely prior to Christianity entering the Americas," I often answer. "Actually, they were Christian long before your own European ancestors first heard the gospel."

My answer often evokes a look of surprise from these questioners. It seems that most people have a simplistic assumption that we have converted from Islam or Judaism. People forget that the message of salvation, crucifixion, and resurrection of our Lord Jesus Christ emanated from Jerusalem. Pentecost took place in Jerusalem.

We, the Christian community of Jerusalem, have a long, unbroken history of faithful witness to the gospel of Jesus. To paraphrase the writer of Hebrews, "We Palestinians have so great a cloud of witnesses" (Hebrews 12:1). Yet for many, it is as if that cloud quickly disintegrated or as if a strong wind blew that cloud far away to the west.[1]

The New Testament Story of the Jerusalem Church

According to the Acts of the Apostles, Jesus commissioned his disciples to be his witnesses—first in Jerusalem, then in Judea and Samaria, then to the ends of the earth (Acts 1:8). They were told to remain in Jerusalem to await the empowering of the Holy Spirit, which came a few days later on Pentecost. The opening chapters of Acts then recount the fascinating story: the witness of the twelve brought unparalleled growth in the Holy City; the followers of the Way demonstrated their love in sharing their resources; signs and wonders complemented the proclamation; and they faced persecution without fear.

The author of Luke-Acts begins in Acts 8 to change the focus from Jerusalem to Judea and Samaria. In chapter 13, the plot shifts to Paul's travels across the Mediterranean westward to "the ends of the earth." However, to suggest that this marks the end to that amazing young congregation in Jerusalem is neither supported by the facts nor does it show confidence in the Holy Spirit's sustaining work.

The Jerusalem community under the leadership of James, the brother of Jesus, continued that faithful witness in the face of hostility while the apostles spread abroad. According to one early historian, James's piety was exemplary: he was known for his "camel knees" because he spent so much time in prayer.[2] The generosity of the community was a factor leading to its poverty, so that Paul's own letters talk of his dedication in taking up an offering for the poor in Jerusalem, lest these mission-ary churches forget how indebted they were to those who shared their spiritual blessings (Romans 15:27).

One also must remember that the canonical writings of the New Testament chose to focus on the spread of Christianity through Paul to the north and to the west. In reality, early Christian missionaries moved out in every direction, including toward Africa and Asia. Those of us with a Palestinian heritage take pride in that cloud of witnesses planted at an early date among Arabs. Already at Pentecost, Acts records the presence of Arabs who heard the disciples speaking in their own language (Acts 2:11). When Paul converted to Christianity several years later, he went to Arabia to be nurtured in the faith (Galatians 1:17). According to our understanding, he went either to one of the Arab-Christian tribes, namely the Nabateans in South Jordan, or to what is now Saudi Arabia. The historian Josephus reported that the Christian community was still going strong in Jerusalem in 67 C.E., and when they left the city during the siege of the Roman general Titus, they found hospitality among the Christians in Pella (Jordan).

The Palestinian Roots in the Early Church

When discussing the New Testament church, I purposely introduce two separate strands, the church in Jerusalem and the church within Arab communities. One cannot separate the two when talking about Palestinian roots. Palestinians are Arabs. Yet it would be a complete misrepresentation to suggest that the Palestinians arrived in the Holy Land only in the seventh century with the migration of Arab tribes. We see our roots going back also to the Canaanites and the Philistines (originally from Crete) who inhabited the land before the arrival of the Israelites under Joshua. It would be simplistic to expect their disappearance from the scene with the establishment of the Israelite monarchy. As is usually the case, indigenous people make efforts to preserve their heritage when dominated by a conquering nation.

Archaeologists tell us that the Holy Land following the time of the exile, and especially at the time of Jesus, had a multicultural character about it. Dwelling alongside the Jewish population were Samaritans, Idumeans (descendants of Esau), Greeks who had come east with the army of Alexander, Roman soldiers, and hosts of other nationalities. Alongside the Jewish temple, there were pagan temples of various kinds. Certainly there was intermarriage. Some non-Jews adopted a Jewish identity. Some Jews adopted non-Jewish identities.

While the Jewish ministry of Jesus is something to be cherished, it would not be right to overlook his openness to those of other backgrounds: the Syrophoenician woman (Mark 7:24-30), the Roman centurion who contributed to the synagogue in Capernaum (Luke 7:1-10), the demoniac from Jerash (Mark 5:1-20), the Samaritan woman at the well (John 4:1-42), and the Greeks in Jerusalem who wished to see Jesus (John 12:20-26). One wonders how much the preservation of their stories in the gospel tradition resulted from the contributions of their families to the early church. When we add the Roman centurion Cornelius, whose story takes up more space than any other convert in the Acts of the Apostles and whose character was exemplified as "a devout man who feared God with all his household" (Acts 10:1), we see that the early Christians in Palestine came to believe very early that "God shows no partiality, but in every nation anyone who fears him and does what is right is acceptable to him" (Acts 10:34). The early church in Jerusalem, which continued to see itself in continuity with Judaism, clearly included also proselytes, "God-fearers," and diaspora Jews. Its diversity is often overlooked because of its conflict with Paul, the apostle to the Gentiles.

We Palestinian Christians see our roots in these early Christians. Over the next centuries, their numbers grew through immigration. Some came from Rome at the time of Jerome, some from Greece and Asia Minor with the rise of the monastic movement, and some from almost every nation through trade and government networks.

These people were Palestinians because they lived in Palestine. Rome, in fact, officially named the region Palestine. What gave Palestinians their Arab identity was that they later adopted the Arab language and culture with the migration of Arab tribes—both Muslim and Christian—to Palestine in the seventh century. Naturally, intermarriage followed, which made the Palestinians Arab by blood. Hence the necessity of describing two different strands of roots for the Palestinian people.

From the New Testament to Constantine

The church historian Eusebius gives a continuous line of fifteen bishops who led the Jerusalem church from the time of James (and his violent death in 62 C.E.).[3] It must have been a vibrant and significant church from his description.

This period was marked by two critical events for Judaism: the destruction of the temple in 70 C.E. and the Bar Kochba revolt from 132 to 135 C.E. The Jewish defeats at the hand of the Romans in both revolts led to the diminished presence of Jews in the Holy Land and to the identity of Christianity as a separate religion. Although a segment of the Jerusalem congregation fled to refuge in Pella during the first revolt, others found safety in the small towns in the surrounding hill country.[4] Afterward, they returned to help rebuild.

According to Eusebius (perhaps an oversimplification), the Jewish-Christian character of the Jerusalem church prevailed until the time of the second revolt. The community suffered at this time because of the messianic claims of the Jewish rebel Bar Kochba. Then, in 135 C.E., the Emperor Hadrian established the new city of Aelia Capitolina in Jerusalem's place, where all circumcised persons were forbidden under a penalty of death. Eusebius notes, however, that Christians continued to be accepted in Jerusalem, seemingly evidence of its diverse character. The line of Jewish-Christian bishops was replaced by those of Gentile origin.

The Palestinian community at this time was distinguished by several leading theologians. Justin from Samaria wrote his important apology for the faith in the early second century before being martyred in Rome. Origen (185–254 C.E.) Pamphilius (240–309 C.E.), and Eusebius (260–340 C.E.), all made Caesarea a leading school of theology. The first of the pilgrims, Bishop Alexander of Cappadocia, came to Jerusalem in 212 C.E. "to worship there and to examine the historic sites."[5]

As a minority, the Christian community was faced with periodic persecution. Under the Roman emperors Decius (249–251 C.E.) and Diocletian (284–305 C.E.), the Christian communities in Palestine were especially singled out, with bishops and clergy being put to death. The situation was so severe that Eusebius devoted a book, *On the Palestinian Martyrs,* to these events.

From Constantine to the Coming of Islam

A turnabout for Christianity in the Roman Empire, and particularly in Palestine, came with the conversion of the Emperor Constantine in 312 C.E. The Nicene Council, attended by Constantine himself, declared Jerusalem to be the mother church of all Christianity in 325 C.E. It ordered that the Temple of Venus, which Hadrian had erected on the site of Golgotha, be torn down. With the help of Helena, the emperor's mother, magnificent churches were built, including the Church of the Holy Sepulchre, the Church of the Nativity in nearby Bethlehem, and one on the Mount of Olives.

Pilgrimages to the Holy Land increased, especially influenced by the journals written by Egeria, who traveled from Spain in the late fourth century, and others. Following the lead of Chariton, who established a monastery in the Jordan Valley and then one south of Bethlehem, people from around the empire chose to adopt the monastic life, so that the Judean desert blossomed with 130 monasteries, including Mar Saba and Saint Theodosius.[6] Hilarion of Gaza promoted the monastic movement in that area. Jerome came from Rome to Bethlehem, where he translated the Bible into Latin. There, he and the noblewoman Paula set up hospices and convents for residents of a deteriorating city of Rome to find refuge. Others from Greece and Asia Minor came to set up support communities for the monasteries. The period was generally marked by theological diversity, with the presence of Syrian, Assyrian, and Armenian communities, as well as those from eastern and western Europe. The best-known bishop of this time, Cyril of Jerusalem, was even considered too conservative in this respect by the local community and was exiled for a period in the 350s C.E.

During this entire period, the church spread throughout the Arab world. Nestorian missionaries promoted the gospel across Mesopotamia and throughout the Persian Gulf region. Arab Christians also participated in formulating the doctrine of the church at the seven ecumenical councils. Among those attending the Nicene Council in 325 C.E. were Bishop Antiochus, the bishop of Capitolias (northern Jordan), and Bishop Cyrenius, the bishop of Amman and Syria. Attending the Council of Ephesus was Bishop Petrus of Bethlehem, known as "the bishop of the tents." One of his disciples was Elijah (494–516 C.E.), the Arab patriarch of Jerusalem. Of the one hundred bishops who attended the Chalcedonian Council in 451 C.E., twenty of them were Arab Christians.[7]

The Arrival of Islam

Islam—a religion also believing in the one God—appeared in the seventh century. Within one generation after the prophet Muhammad, Jerusalem was under Muslim rule. In some ways, it seems strange that Arab Christians welcomed the Muslim invasions. However, there had been a backlash to get rid of Byzantine control, which had tried to suffocate any culture or language other than Greek. Jerusalem had suffered greatly under the Persian conquest of 614 and then under a Byzantine resurgence in 628. The arrival of the Caliph Omar in 637 seemed to many Jerusalem Christians to be an attractive alternative. Patriarch Sophronius peacefully handed over the keys to the city.[8]

Generally, Christians fared well under Muslim control, for a number of reasons. First, the prophet Muhammad had developed the concept of the People of the Book *(Ahl al-Kitab)*. The common heritage of Muslims, Christians, and Jews was something to be treasured. As a result, good relationships predominated.

Second, the system of *Ahl al-Dhimma* was introduced. Muslims had the duty to protect non-Muslim groups and their members *(dhimmi)*, and, in exchange, non-Muslims were obliged to submit to the Muslim regime, including payment of taxes *(al-Jizyeh)*.[9] This tolerant system allowed Arab Christians to participate actively to an important degree in all aspects of life, on condition that they did so under the control and within the jurisdiction of Muslim order. The Arab Christians made many contributions to the Muslim empire. They developed the rules of administration in Iraq and Egypt. They strengthened the economy and organized the system of taxation in Egypt, in particular. The geographer Muqaddasi in 985 described Jerusalem as a city of *dhimmis:* "Everywhere the Jews and the Christians have the upper hand."[10] For

the Christians, they were the privileged class, including the best educated and the wealthiest.

Caliph Omar arrived with a positive attitude toward Christianity. In
fact, two Arab-Christian tribes had accompanied him, and they chose to
settle in the region around Bethlehem.[11] The famous encounter between
Caliph Omar and Patriarch Sophronius seems to have set the tone for
Muslim–Christian interaction. According to the story, the patriarch was
guiding Omar through the Church of the Holy Sepulchre when the time
for Muslim prayer came. Sophronius welcomed him to pray within the
church itself. Omar declined, expressing concern that some might want
to change the church into a mosque. He respectfully retreated outside
to say his prayers. Today, not far from the Lutheran church in the Old
City, the mosque of Omar commemorates that encounter. Omar recipro-
cated by offering a document known as the Covenant of Omar, which
offered his personal guarantee of safety and protection for Christians,
their property, and their churches. This guarantee steered normal relations between the two religions away from confrontation and toward
coexistence.

There were, to be sure, moments of conflict. Much later, persecution
became the norm under the Mamelukes (1293–1354). Many also cite as
evidence the regime of Caliph al-Hakim (996–1021), when Christians
were persecuted and the Church of the Holy Sepulchre was destroyed.
Others note, however, al-Hakim's dementia and unacceptable claims to
be Allah incarnate.[12] Some argue that Christians were treated with hostility from the beginning, pointing to the archaeological evidence of
numerous destroyed and abandoned churches and monasteries in the
eighth century. That evidence is indisputable, but its interpretation is
debatable. Was it the result of a violent conquest? Other factors must
also be considered, including a devastating earthquake in 747 and a subsequent plague that depopulated the cities. Why place blame on the Muslims? In fact, when the Persians destroyed the Church of the Resurrection
in Jerusalem, Muslims encouraged Christians to gather offerings for its
reconstruction.

One does see a clear shift from Byzantine Greek culture—itself foreign to Palestinian soil—to Islamic Arab ways. Primary was the adoption
of the Arabic language. The monasteries of Mar Saba and Saint Cather-
ine's in the Sinai house great collections of Arabic manuscripts from the
eighth century, demonstrating a flourishing of Arab-Christian literature.[13]
In many cases, Arabization also meant Islamization, especially among

Christian tribes in rural areas. A case in point is the community of Abeddya, not far from Jerusalem. The Arabic name of the town notes the residents' historic role as servants—like the Old Testament name Obadiah. Centuries before the Arabs' arrival, Greek-speaking Christian immigrants from Asia Minor came to provide support for nearby Saint Theodosius monastery. Today, the village is entirely Muslim. When this change occurred, no one knows. Probably through a gradual process of assimilation, the Greek-Christian community adopted the Arabic language, then Arabic culture, and eventually Islam. In such a way, Christian numbers in the Holy Land declined.

Still, Arab-Christian theologians continued to flourish in dialogue with Islam. Where Greek-oriented doctrinal statements concerning the nature of God and of Christ clashed directly with Muslim monotheism, Palestinian theology bridged the gap for fruitful discussion. Familiar illustrations for the Trinity, such as the sun with its beams of light and heat, first originated in these discussions. John of Damascus made his home at the Mar Saba monastery where he defended the Christian use of images, wrote magnificent hymns, and produced a host of theological treatises.[14]

Arab Christians played a strong cultural and societal role in the Abbasid reign. Christians were employed in key financial and professional positions. The caliphs' great open-mindedness created groups of translators who became well known around 830 as the famous *Beit al-Hikma*,[15] the House of Knowledge. The translation of Greek philosophy and other sciences proceeded at an accelerated rate to make Baghdad, under Haroun al-Rashid, a capital without peer in the medieval world. Al-Farabi (the philosopher known as the second Aristotle), Yihya ibn Adi (who also wrote about the trinity and soteriology), the physician and philosopher Abū al-Faraj ibn 'Abdallāh al-Tayyib (d. 1043), and other Arab Christians contributed to the Golden Age of Islam while Europe groped through its Dark Ages.

The Crusader Period

When apocalyptic fears and rumors concerning the end of the world grew at the turn of the twelfth century, many in Europe turned their eyes eastward. The Crusades are commonly described as the European church's attempt to capture back the Holy Land from the "infidel." The problem is that Arab Christians had never left. We had never lost it. The

Europeans were frustrated in their unsuccessful campaign with Islam in places like Spain and southern France, and they projected it all upon us.

One only had to travel with the crusaders (1099–1292) as far as Constantinople to understand their purpose. They sacked the Christian city and deposed the Greek Orthodox patriarch. Their enemy was not Islam, but anything "Eastern."

The slaughter that occurred in Jerusalem has been documented with all its gory details.[16] The conquerors attacked everyone who looked Middle Eastern and spoke a different language. Neither were they satisfied with taking the city of Jerusalem. The entire village of Beit Jala—at that time completely Christian—was annihilated. The story can be repeated throughout the region. No wonder the Christians did not welcome the crusaders. No wonder they took up arms against them.

Baldwin was enthroned as crusader king of Jerusalem in a religious ceremony in Bethlehem's Church of the Nativity. Latin Christianity was declared to be the only accepted religion. Jews and Muslims were denied residency. Arab and other eastern Christians were also banned from the city of Jerusalem, including the Greek Orthodox patriarch. Eventually Syriac, Armenian, and Orthodox communities were allowed to practice their religion, but only under Latin authority.

The crusaders left their mark on Jerusalem with impressive architecture and with the establishment of new commemorative Christian sites (often chosen for convenience' sake rather than historical accuracy). However, the dominant legacy left by the crusaders on the Arab psyche is a deep suspicion of Western military and colonial interests. Whether it is nineteenth-century Christian missionary movements, or the twentieth-century immigration of Jews from Europe, or even recent American political and economic activities—all such efforts are still today viewed with suspicion. Have the Crusades ever really come to an end?

Salah al-Din, a Kurdish military general, is given credit for liberating Jerusalem in 1187 shortly after his famous victory at the Horns of Hattim in Galilee. For some, this is interpreted as a Muslim victory against the Christian crusaders. The truth is that Middle Eastern Christians fought at Salah al-Din's side. Two of his leading generals were Christians.

Salah al-Din had given an order to spare the lives of the Latin-Christian residents of Jerusalem. He kept it. At first, his soldiers rounded up many of these Christians to sell into slavery. A story relates how he was moved to tears when he saw families divided up in this process, and large numbers were released. When some of his military criticized him for allowing great wealth to be taken from the city, he refused to change his mind, saying, "Christians everywhere will remember the kindness we have done them."[17]

Under the crusaders, Jerusalem's Christian population had swelled to sixty thousand, according to some sources. With the departure of so many Latin Christians, Salah al-Din wanted to assure the continuation of this city's grandeur. The Greek Orthodox were given full protection, and their churches were restored. Under his successors, Christians were encouraged to rebuild homes and to build new churches. Additional Christian communities were welcomed and officially recognized in Jerusalem, including the Armenians and Syriacs, the Copts and Ethiopians.

Perhaps the Muslim Salah al-Din's most significant decision was to invite Jews to live in Jerusalem for the first time since the Roman ban in 135 C.E.

Ottoman Rule

From 1517 to 1918, the Holy Land was under the rule of the Ottoman Empire based in Turkey. Much of the structure of modern Jerusalem was shaped during this time. In 1536, the Sultan Suleiman the Magnificent fortified the city by constructing the walls that still encompass the Old City today, and he established its strategic water system.

More importantly, Christian–Muslim relations became institutionalized in what became known as the *millet* system.[18] This system recognized the different sects, churches, and religious communities as "autonomous" for governing themselves in civil and religious matters. The head of a church or sect was considered to be the leader and spokesperson for his church and community in matters related to the civil authorities. The Greek Orthodox patriarch, for example, was the officially recognized spokesperson for the Christian community. To a degree, this system still operates today in the Middle East, including Israel.

The organization of Jerusalem into Quarters according to religious communities was part of this system. At the beginning of the Ottoman period, the influence of Christianity had diminished. The Christian population of Jerusalem numbered about 1,650, less than 15 percent of the total population.[19] Its strength was in the small towns and villages of the countryside.

The political intrigues of Europe continued to affect the Holy Land. The Ottomans made agreements known as *Capitulations*, which gave European countries limited jurisdiction within the Ottoman Empire. *Capitulations* with France thus paved the way for Catholic missionaries to play an important role in the Holy Land. Their success can be measured by the increase in the Christian population in Jerusalem to 2,750 by 1800, at a time when the total population had decreased by half since 1553.[20] At the same time, Greek Catholic, Syriac Catholic, Armenian Catholic, and Maronite Catholic churches were formed, retaining Eastern liturgies but declaring unity with Rome.

Because of an appreciation for the humble character of St. Francis of Assisi, Franciscans in particular were granted special privileges. *Capitulations* were established in 1604 to give the Franciscans the role of protectors of the Holy Places, a status they retain today.

These external political agreements set the stage for division among Jerusalem Christians. The Ottoman *millet* system gave the Greek Orthodox patriarch one kind of authority, while the *Capitulations* with Europeans gave the Franciscans another.

In 1808, a fire broke out in the Church of the Holy Sepulchre that gutted the entire structure. Each of the six denominations of churches that controlled sections of the building blamed the other. The privilege of rebuilding was—to put it bluntly—auctioned off by the Ottomans to the highest bidder, in this case, the Greek Orthodox. While this increased their "ownership," they also took advantage to remove signs of Franciscan influence. The Greek Orthodox now controlled Golgotha and the tomb of Christ, while Franciscans, Syrians, Copts, and Armenians were restricted to small chapels.[21] The Ethiopians were removed to the rooftop. The keys of the church were given for safekeeping to a Muslim family, who to this day have the responsibility of locking and unlocking the church.

For half a century, inter-Christian conflict in the Jerusalem area simmered until it actually led to the outbreak of the Crimean War in 1854. The spark came from a bloody brawl between Orthodox and Catholic priests in Bethlehem's Church of the Nativity over the disappearance of the silver star marking the birthplace of Jesus. With Russia taking the side of the Orthodox, France and Britain declared war to stop Russia from using this pretext to invade Ottoman territory. One result of the French and British victory was the *Status Quo* arrangement, which regulated the rights and privileges of the various churches to worship at the different Holy Places, such as the Holy Sepulchre and the Church of the Nativity in Bethlehem. This arrangement is still in force.

As Ottoman power decreased in the nineteenth century, further political dealings brought interest from other European countries, especially England and Germany. This paved the way for a revival of pilgrimage and the new archaeological studies of the Holy Land and its historical sites. Increasing immigration swelled the population of Jerusalem so that new settlements cropped up outside the city walls, including the German, Russian, and American colonies and significant Jewish communities.

The evangelical movement came to Jerusalem at this time, primarily Anglicans and Lutherans.[22] In 1841, a joint evangelical bishopric was given official sanction with the position of bishop alternating between Anglicans and Lutherans. The Englishman appointed as the first bishop, Michael Solomon, was a Jewish convert who built Christ Church Cathedral next to the British consulate near the Jaffa Gate. His announced strategy was to target the Jews for evangelism.

When it was the Prussian Lutherans' turn, Bishop Gobat chose a different strategy. The church was to provide a social ministry including hospitals and schools—one for Jewish converts and another for Arab Christians. This program was developed further by the Swabian missionary Johann Ludwig Schneller, who developed the well-respected Schneller School for boys west of the Old City. In 1860, he brought ten orphans from the area that is now Lebanon to launch the Syrian Orphanage for young people from throughout the region (known then as Greater Syria), both Christian and Muslim. At the same time, the *Kaiserwerth* focused on diaconia (ministry of service, as deacons) and instituted the Talitha Kumi School for girls.

With Anglicans and Lutherans taking different approaches, the bishopric separated into two after the thirteenth joint appointment. Christ Church continues its particular mission to Jews. However, the Anglican church as a whole began to concentrate increasingly on mission among Arabs and on building schools and hospitals. In 1869, the Turkish sultan gave the Prussian king a plot of land in the heart of the Old City not far from the Holy Sepulchre. There, Kaiser Wilhelm II built the Lutheran Church of the Redeemer, dedicated in 1898. Other Lutheran congregations were established in Bethlehem and Hebron.

The evangelicals made an impact on Christian life in Jerusalem and throughout the Middle East. Presbyterians were active in Lebanon, but not in Jerusalem. Anglicans contributed in several locations. Lutherans centered on Jerusalem. Through hospitals, schools, and various social agencies, they improved the quality of life, and the cultural revival promoted individual faith. In Lebanon, the whole Bible was translated into Arabic for the first time in 1864. Printing presses published newspapers and Arabic literature.[23]

The impact of evangelicals was perhaps strongest in Lebanon. There, the movement toward Pan-Arabism began. The Ottoman government had emphasized smaller localities, placing everyone in their own box. Evangelicals such as Bustrus al-Bustani, known for his literary accomplishment, began to question this arrangement. How do we get out? How do we reach beyond boundaries to unite the Arab world and to speak to universal Arab concerns? In a sense, then, this was the beginning of democratic thinking in the Middle East.

The success of Palestinian Christians and their achievements in education had another effect. During the last twenty-five years of the Ottoman Empire, many began looking for opportunities elsewhere. An estimated 350,000 Christians from Greater Syria, a good portion of them Palestinians, emigrated to North and South America.[24]

The Twentieth Century

Arabs eagerly heeded the West's call to throw off the Ottoman yoke during World War I. The British had promised them self-determination and self-rule in return for their cooperation. Instead, for Palestinian Christians and Muslims, a century of European intervention and of Palestinian devastation followed, first with establishment of the British Mandate in 1918 and then with the state of Israel in 1948.

While the Jewish population of Palestine had increased gradually from only 5 percent of the total in 1881 under the Ottoman Empire to 8 percent at the beginning of the British Mandate, it rose dramatically to 32 percent by the end of World War II. This represented an increase for Jews of 2,200 percent in actual population in sixty-four years. The Muslim population more than doubled during this period due to natural growth. The Christian population fared much worse, increasing only 1.8 percent, partly due to increased emigration at the end of Ottoman rule. Christians accounted for 15 percent of the population in 1881 but dropped to 7.5 percent by 1944. Today, it is estimated that

Population of Palestine[25]

Year	Muslims	Jews	Christians
1881	400,000	25,000	75,000
1918	574,000	56,000	70,000
1922	589,177	83,790	88,907
1931	759,700	174,606	93,500
1939	797,133	445,457	116,958
1944	1,061,277	553,600	135,547

Christians make up only 1.9 percent of the combined Israeli and Palestinian population.

The Christian presence in Jerusalem has endured through the centuries. While it has never constituted a majority since crusader times, its population generally ranged from 15 percent to 38 percent of the city's residents prior to the establishment of the state of Israel. That figure has diminished significantly in recent years, so that the actual number of Christians is now comparable to the number in 1900 (considering natural growth rates, the figure today should be seventy thousand or more), and the proportion has dropped to 4 percent of the total population. Nevertheless, Jerusalem Christians still see themselves as the salt of the earth.

This role can be demonstrated through the influence of Christian schools—Catholic, Maronite, and Evangelical—that fostered a new generation with both spiritual and nationalistic identity. Such prominent Christians as Nasif al-Yaziji, Faris al-Shidyaq, and Bustrus al-Bustani established the Arabic literary renaissance.[27] They also played a creative role in the development of Arab nationalist thought. These were important currents in the movement toward the new Arabization of the church in the Holy Land and the whole of the Middle East. The efforts and intellectual contributions of these Christians (including the later work of Michel Aflaq, the Syrian founder of the Ba'ath movement)[28] emphasized the Arab nationalistic inclinations of indigenous Arab Christians. Pan-Arab nationalism united Christians and Muslims in one framework. It launched the idea of working together for a societal and political project that was broader than the *millet* system and that was all-encompassing. The Arab nationalism initiated by Arab Christians,

Jerusalem Population[26]

Year	Total	Christian	Jewish	Muslim
1553	13,384	1,650	1,650	10,084
1850	15,000	3,650	6,000	5,350
1880	31,000	6,000	17,000	8,000
1900	55,000	10,000	35,000	10,000
1922	62,600	14,700	34,400	13,500
1945	73,000	28,000	18,000	27,000
1989*	282,573	11,767	140,000	130,733

*This reflects extended boundaries for Jerusalem after the 1967 War.

among others, promoted a citizenship built not on the claims of religion but on the basis of equality in all the rights and duties.

Since the Pentecost gathering reported in Acts 2, the Christian community has played a significant, unbroken role in Jerusalem and in Palestine. The last century, however, saw the church becoming an endangered species. The accompanying charts demonstrate how European anti-Semitism led to a gradual but significant increase in Jewish population throughout the first half of the century. In the last fifty years, however, the establishment of the state of Israel has had such an effect that Christians have dropped to only 1.9 percent of the population.

These events have been described in books, which makes it unnecessary to go through all the details here. Don Wagner's *Dying in the Land of Promise*[29] gives an excellent interpretation. However, it is important to note particularly how the events of 1947–48 affected the Christian community.

At the outset, the 1947 United Nations plan to partition Palestine cannot be considered a fair resolution of the situation. One-third of the population (the Jews) was to receive 54 percent of the land. Nevertheless, it did include two positive aspects. First, Palestinians would have been given self-rule. Second, under the international status of a greater Jerusalem, the Christian community, and the Lutheran community in particular, would have fared well. However, the partition plan was not implemented by the UN.[30]

The textbook explanation is that seven Arab armies attacked Israel on May 15, 1948, the day after Israel had declared independence.

Land Ownership

Year	Arab	Jewish	Church
1914	98%	2%	10%
1946	95%	5%	10%

Jewish Control of Land in Palestine

1947	54%	UN Partition Plan
1948	78%	Armistice at end of 1948 War
1967	100%	End of 1967 War
1995	98%	Oslo Peace Accords

According to the usual interpretation, the Arabs are to blame. As a Palestinian, I tell you that this is a myth—and not only in my opinion. A new wave of research by Israeli historians has documented that much of the story painted in the West does not measure up to reality.[31]

The war did not begin in 1948 but shortly after the UN vote on partition in November 1947, when Israeli militias called the Haganah, Irgun, and the Stern gang began attacking Arab communities within the newly drawn borders of Israel. In those six months, before a single Iraqi or Jordanian tank had crossed the Jordan River, the Israelis had accomplished two important goals: they had expelled over a half million Arabs from their homes, and they had conquered half of greater Jerusalem. By the time the armistices were signed, they had added a third— an additional 24 percent of Palestinian land.

As a result, Israel controlled of 78 percent of the land, the remaining 22 percent was annexed to Jordan as the West Bank (and Gaza was placed under Egyptian control), and Jerusalem itself became a divided city. Palestinians controlled nothing. This is why we Palestinians refer to the 1948 war as *al-Nakba,* the "Catastrophe."

What was the impact particularly on the Christian community? First, we became a refugee church. Among all the refugees in 1948, fifty thousand were Christian families, many from the towns of Jaffa, Lydda, Ramle, and throughout the Galilee.[32] A significant portion came also from the western part of Jerusalem. Thirty-five percent of the Christians in the Holy Land became refugees. Monasteries and churches opened their doors to provide housing for families, and relief agencies provided care. Our own Augusta Victoria Hospital changed its mission to provide health care for refugees.

Second, the church lost major holdings. Not only were there many wealthy Christian families in western Jerusalem and the many destroyed villages, but the church itself was a large landowner. The whole area where the Israeli Knesset and the Israel Museum are located was a tract of land owned by the Greek Orthodox Church. The Latin Patriarchate and the Armenians had landholdings going back centuries; the Lutheran church lost the Schneller School and then landholdings.

The church in the Holy Land became divided, because there were also Palestinians remaining in Israel proper. The Israeli Arab population has continued to grow, so that today they number 1,300,000, including Christians living in towns like Nazareth and Ramle. After 1949, they no longer were allowed to cross the international border to the Holy Places in East Jerusalem.

The 1967 War completed the Catastrophe. The West Bank, the rest of Jerusalem, and Gaza all were occupied by Israel. There was a new flood of refugees. The church lost more landholdings in East Jerusalem. Because of the political and economic instability since 1967, a significant number of Christian families have chosen to emigrate. The average age of Christians in the Holy Land today is thirty-two—double the average age of Palestinians in general. Unless something changes, the churches in Jerusalem could one day become empty museums.

The Evangelical Lutheran Church in Jerusalem

The church struggled under very difficult conditions during the latter part of the twentieth century. Because of this, its witness has an even greater impact.

In death, there is life. In pain, there is birth. The Evangelical Lutheran Church in Jordan (ELCJ) was born during this difficult period. In 1959, Lutheran congregations chose to organize as an independent church affiliated with the Lutheran World Federation. The name was chosen because at that time all the congregations were located within the state of Jordan. One congregation was located in the Old City of Jerusalem. Three, with roots in nineteenth-century evangelical work, were in the

Bethlehem area: Beit Jala, Beit Sahour, and Bethlehem.[33] Two were refugee congregations: one in Ramallah and one in Amman.

The ELCJ has established an impressive and well-respected system of schools. Today there are three thousand children in five schools. According to the statistics of 1998/1999, 6 percent of our students are Lutherans, 31 percent are Muslims, and the others are from the various churches.[34] Augusta Victoria Hospital provides high-quality medical care, now with a specialty in cancer treatment. Our church offers a variety of social programs, youth work, and women's programs.

From our offices in Jerusalem's Church of the Redeemer, we continue to minister to pilgrims, to provide education and interpretation. Ministries in the English, German, and Danish languages for expatriates are also provided at the Redeemer Church. Other church partners carry out Lutheran ministry in Finnish, Swedish, and Norwegian at various centers.

To establish itself as Lutheran, the church entrusted me with the task of translating the Augsburg Confession into Arabic. To establish itself as fully Palestinian, church leadership was expected to be Palestinian. There have now been three Palestinian bishops of the ELCJ: from 1979, Daoud Haddad; from 1986, Naim Nasser; and from 1998, Munib Younan.

We are surrounded with a great cloud of witnesses. For two thousand years, the church has provided a constant, powerful witness to the world in Jerusalem. It has had its ups and its downs. Yet, it has never become discouraged and has never despaired. It has been faithful to its heritage.

The witness began with Jesus commissioning his disciples on the nearby Mount of Olives. That witness traveled to Judea, Samaria, and to the ends of the earth. Two thousand years later, the witness continues in Jerusalem.

2

"We Have This Cloud of Witnesses," II

The Younan Family Story

As Palestinians, we have a cloud of witnesses who go back to the early church. As a family, I have a cloud of witnesses who have shaped and nurtured me for my ministry in the church.

My name is Munib Andria Munib Younan. The Palestinian custom is to take the father's name as the middle name. The grandfather's name is retained as a second middle name. My name, father's name, grandfather's name, family name. So, my father was named Andria and my grandfather Munib. In such a way, we express the importance and the continuity of family. My son is Andria Munib Andria Younan. A daughter gets the father's first name and the grandfather's name. So my daughters are Anna Liza Munib Andria Younan and Martha Munib Andria Younan.

The Origin of the Younan Family in Beersheba

The Younan family is not very large. The name Younan means "Greek." How far back does it go? We have no way of knowing. Nothing is written. My father used to talk about old family legends that claim we once were a rather well-to-do family with landholdings and olive groves near Athens. At some point—what century, we don't know—one of my ancestors visited the Holy Land as a pilgrim. When his sister died in Gaza, he was too ashamed to return to Greece. So he married a Palestinian woman and moved to Beersheba in southern Palestine. We have relatives in Gaza, so perhaps a brother remained there as well.

Why are we called Younan? Either this grandfather did not speak Arabic, and they said about him, "Younan," or his name had been

Johannis, and the Arabs could not pronounce Johannis. These are the legends about the name, but I don't know. How far back they go I don't know. We have tried to find the record in books but can locate nothing.

Genealogically, one cannot be 100 percent sure where Palestinians originated. Jews married Muslims and became Muslims. Christians married Jews and became Jews. Many immigrated here in the sixteenth to eighteenth centuries to find work under the Turks when Europe was boiling. They became Palestinians, fully Palestinians.

We have a very interesting history. My father came from Beersheba. It seems that my grandfather was a well-to-do person. He was a merchant of seeds and grains, and he apparently sold quite a lot of his products to the occupying Turkish army. He was also known for playing the trombone. As far as we know, he was a religious man. Every Sunday he prayed. He wouldn't leave the services early. He and I, of course, share the name Munib, which is actually a common name for the eldest child. It's a Qur'anic name, meaning either "the representative," "a man sent by God," or "a servant of God." So it fit his religious personality well. My grandfather also had difficulties, because my grandmother passed away in 1936 when he was only about forty years old. Then he married a second time.

My grandfather took care that my father was educated in the Evangelical Alliance school in Beersheba. It no longer exists, of course, but he was educated in that tradition. He was a seeker, and he wanted to become a missionary—someone who went around from home to home passing out Bibles and tracts, someone who called people to salvation. He was a good reader, and I got a lot of Arabic theological books from him.

My mother's family was from the western part of Jerusalem. She studied in the Talitha Kumi School when it was located on King George Street in Jerusalem (today it is in Beit Jala). When I look at her, I realize the quality of education that was offered in the Lutheran schools. She speaks very good English and very good German to this day. At the Talitha Kumi School, she also came to have a strong evangelical faith. It seems that my father and my mother met on the evangelical basis. There were a lot of differences between them—my father was at least ten years older. I have wondered many times, What brought them together? Was it their common Christian commitment and evangelical spirit? She got it from Talitha Kumi and he from the Evangelical Alliance. This speaks well of the Christian schools.

A Family of Refugees

One very important element in my history is that we are a family of refugees. All sides of my family and my wife's family were affected drastically by the Catastrophe of 1948.

My father was a refuge from Beersheba who came to Jerusalem for safety during that period just before the armistice, when the Haganah was attacking Arab communities to expand Jewish landholdings. According to the UN partition plan, the city of Beersheba had been attached to the southwest portion of Palestine. This made perfect sense, because Jews constituted only 1 percent of the Beersheba district. However, it was located on an important crossroads. By May 1948, the Haganah had captured three nearby Arab villages.[1] During the second truce in the war (beginning July 1948), the Israeli army planned and launched a major offensive called Operation *Yo'av* to gain control of territory along the south and west that had been assigned to Palestine. The residents of Beersheba, however, managed to resist until October 1948, when the city fell into Israeli hands. Sixty-five hundred Arab residents were forced to leave, including the Younan family. In early 1949, when the armistice was signed with Arab nations, Beersheba was now part of Israel. The previous inhabitants were not allowed to return. So, 1948 marked the end of the Christian community in Beersheba. Even the graves from my grandfather's time are gone. Likely our home is still standing, because many were taken over by Israeli families. Yet, that is something I really don't know.

As for my mother, her home was in the western part of Jerusalem on Mandelbaum Street. That story is well known. Her family assumed, as did many Christian families, that Jerusalem was to be an international city with protection guaranteed by the world community. Yet, beginning already in 1947, the underground Irgun, led by future Israeli Prime Minister Menachem Begin, began attacking Arab communities. An attack on December 13, 1947, in residential sections left several dozen dead. On January 5, the Haganah blew up the Semiramis Hotel in another residential section, killing twenty civilians. And so it went. By April 30, 1948—two weeks before the declaration of Israel's independence and before the entry of Arab armies—all Palestinian neighborhoods in West Jerusalem had been militarily occupied, and all Arab residents had been driven out.[2]

My mother describes her experience as if it happened yesterday. The Haganah drove up and down the streets with loudspeakers blaring instructions that all Arabs were to leave their houses for their own protection. The Haganah promised that it would only be a temporary leave—two weeks at most. Quickly, my mother and her neighbors gathered up whatever belongings they could carry in a suitcase and left. Only three minutes later, as she was making her way toward the Old City, there was a loud explosion. Turning, they could see smoke rising from her very own home. It had received a direct hit by a shell. Her entire neighborhood would soon be leveled to the ground. In a matter of minutes, her whole life had changed.

For quite some time, they held out hope of some kind of a restoration, if not by military force, then by negotiation. As late as September 16, 1949, UN mediator Count Bernadotte proposed a new partition of Palestine, including the internationalization of Jerusalem and return or compensation for refugees. The following day he was murdered in Jerusalem, apparently by the extreme Zionist Stern gang. Then it became obvious that Jerusalem would be a divided city, and there would be no return.

My wife Suad's family is from Kufor Bir'im on the border with Lebanon. Father Elias Chacour made the story of the village famous in *Blood Brothers*.[3] The history of this place goes back to Canaanite times, when its name was Periy'am. Nineteenth-century accounts of the village describe it as a pleasant place to live, with stone houses surrounded by gardens, vineyards, and olive groves. By 1945, there were about 150 houses and the population was 710, almost entirely Christian.[4]

Father Chacour describes how his and other families showed hospitality to Jews coming to the area following the Holocaust. They were moved by the immigrants' stories and could not believe how anyone would have treated them as the Nazis did. The villagers had no concern that their lives would change. The UN partition plan of 1947 had designated northern Galilee with its high Arab population as part of the anticipated Palestinian state.

However, Israel's new prime minister, David Ben-Gurion, announced to his cabinet that Galilee would become "clean" and "empty" of Arabs.[5] This was carried out by Operation Hiram—a sixty-hour campaign from October 29 to 31, 1948, designed, according to a *New York Times* article, "to eliminate the Arab-held bulge descending into Galilee from Lebanon."[6] On the night of October 30, area villages were bombed, including Jish just two miles to the southwest, and a horrible massacre took place in Safsaf. Still, the villagers trusted the Israeli army when they were told to leave their homes "temporarily" for "security reasons." Some hid in caves, others went to the now-deserted village of Jish, still others traveled north into Lebanon. None were ever allowed to return to their home village. Families were split because those heading north were never allowed back into Israel. When the armistice lines were drawn, Bir'im and surrounding villages were part of Israel.

Unlike my father and mother, who had fled to Jerusalem's Old City and were thus forbidden by Israeli law to return to their homes, my wife's father was still within the newly established borders of Israel. He was given Israeli citizenship. He and other Bir'im residents, therefore, tried to use the legal system to retrieve their land and homes. The case went to the Israeli Supreme Court, which ruled in their favor, stating that they should be allowed to return to their homes in Bir'im by December 1953. The villagers packed their bags and made the hike in order to be home by Christmas. However, the Israeli army had other plans. In spite of the court ruling, they bombed the village so that not a single home was left standing. When the villagers arrived, not only did they face this utter disappointment, but they were once again expelled from the land, which was then allotted to the new Kibbutz Bara'am.[7]

My father-in-law eventually settled in Haifa, where he married my mother-in-law from the Hawa family of Nazareth, and together they raised a family. I should mention that Nazareth also had originally been designated by the UN partition plan to be part of the Palestinian state. It was captured by Israel in July 1948, just before a truce was signed. As a result, my wife, Suad, and her family are among the 1.3 million Arabs who have Israeli citizenship.

When I say that I come from a family of refugees, it is three times over. Our family story illustrates the tragedy of the years 1947–48, which the Israelis call the War of Independence and we call the Catastrophe—*al Nakba*.

On December 11, 1948, the UN General Assembly passed Resolution 194 stating "that the refugees wishing to return to their homes and live in peace with their neighbours should be permitted to do so at the earliest practical date, and that compensation should be paid for the property of those choosing not to return." That settlement was never reached. On November 17, 1949, the chairman of the UN Conciliation Commission for Palestine wrote a letter to the secretary-general describing the stark condition of the refugees and recommending the establishment of the United Nations Relief and Works Agency (UNRWA), which to this day provides assistance to the 750,000 refugees and their families. Again on November 22, 1967, the UN Security Council Resolution 242 called "for achieving a just settlement of the refugee problem."

I've thought many times, if I had lived in a refugee camp, would I have become a pastor or bishop? Or if I had lived there, would I have joined freedom fighters, or a military wing? I do not know. Thanks to the church that embraced me and my family I have become what I have become. Life for most of the refugees has been extremely difficult, even more difficult than my life in Jerusalem. I carry a refugee card to remind me of my status and to affirm my identification with all of these many families. Some have suggested to me that since I am now a bishop, this is unnecessary. For me, it is a matter of my roots. I am a Palestinian bishop who is a refugee.

Growing up in the Old City

When Israel took over western Jerusalem in early 1948, my mother's family fled to the Old City. Everywhere they went, there were people seeking temporary shelter. The Armenian convent was crowded. The Lutheran Church of the Redeemer housed about fifteen groups.

My mother found a place along with fifteen other families in the Greek Orthodox convent of John the Baptist, very close to the Lutheran church. The compound is totally surrounded by a brick wall with an entrance hidden between shops on Christian Quarter Road, not far from David Street where people turn to walk uphill to Jaffa Gate.

Even today, the doorway is so small that a person has to bend in order to enter. Straight ahead is the church, a very simple domed structure. Through the summer months of 1948, the Israeli army tried to extend its Jerusalem holdings. My mother relates how the refugees would squeeze together in the church basement during the attacks, often fifty or more people at a time. The Orthodox priests told her that John the Baptist's parents, Zechariah and Elizabeth, had once lived there, and that Zechariah often went to the temple, where he served as a priest, through a long tunnel underneath the streets of the city. Whether or not that was true, she did not know. The stories helped to pass the time and to understand our roots—that we belonged.

There were several wells in the courtyard surrounding the church. Around the perimeter, people constructed makeshift dwellings. They held out hope that they would one day return to their old neighborhoods. "As soon as the fighting stops," they all said. "The Jews are reasonable people. It is only a matter of time." However, months extended into years, and still there was no solution. The makeshift dwellings became permanent. The promised "two weeks" never ended.

Shortly after they came to the Old City, my parents married. Our house was up some stairs, bordering on David Street. It was small, but we had a home. It is painful to remember and to relive those days because we were a poor family. I recall sometimes as a child not having anything to eat. This was the situation even though my parents were human, and they were ready to do anything. I remember my first jacket. My father took his old jacket to the tailor and for half a dinar—which was quite a bit of money—had it made small enough for me. But I'm proud of this.

I remember when I was attending the Lutheran school, and my father used to argue with my mother because they could not afford to pay the half-dinar tuition fee. He was always telling her, "You are spoiling our children. Take them out of school. Let Munib [because I was the eldest] become a plumber, and thus he could assist me in earning a living for this house." I was at that time ten years old, but my mother wouldn't let him. He simply looked at her and said, "Yes, yes, yes." So my father allowed me to be educated.

Eventually my mother, too, found a job cleaning at the Lutheran church in order to meet our tuition fees and pay for our needs. Of course, we realized what she was doing and appreciated it. There were five children (two brothers—Maurice and Michael—and twin girls—Margaret and Marcelle), and she wanted us all to receive a good education. My father was working very hard, but for too little money. By then, he was already in his fifties, and the physical labor was beginning to be difficult for him. So, my mother came to work at the Lutheran church, and she always told us that to work was nothing to be ashamed of. It is better than to beg for the sake of our education.

Spiritual Upbringing

My parents were married in the Greek Orthodox Church, and they baptized all of us children in the Orthodox church. Yet, from the very beginning, my parents wanted us to grow up in the Lutheran tradition. Of course, my mother had gone to the Lutheran Talitha Kumi School. There had been no Lutheran churches in Beersheba, but my father had been raised in the Evangelical Alliance. In Jerusalem, he occasionally attended the Anglican church and other times went to services at Redeemer along with my mother. Nevertheless, they always considered themselves Orthodox. As for us children, it was understood that we would be raised Lutheran.

My parents agreed that we would best learn the right theology in the Lutheran schools. There were certainly other options, and cheaper ones. To the Orthodox, my father said no; to the Anglican, he said no. My parents had determined that we would be educated in the Lutheran schools. At first, it was the old Martin Luther School, next to the Lutheran church near our home. Actually, it was then known as the Adda Bhaghda School, from earlier times when Muristan Road was called "Leather Workers Street." The school adopted the name Martin Luther School in 1962. That is where I began my education. Then, at age eleven, I was sent to boarding school at Beit Jala. Boys and girls were educated separately; the Talitha Kumi School had been relocated to Beit Jala as a girls' school in 1959. What I remember best from my five years there were the long hikes we would take on weekends. I got to know every inch of the hills throughout the region south of Jerusalem. As I grew up, I fell in love with the land.

Sometimes it was lonely being away from my family. Yet my parents never accepted that I should change it. They said, "We want you to have this." So naturally, I accepted confirmation after taking classes at the boarding section of the school. It was with my parents' counsel, not against their will. They wanted this for all my brothers and sisters, to be confirmed in the Lutheran church.

Our home in Jerusalem was a place for Bible study every Tuesday afternoon from 3:30 to 5:00 P.M. for anyone who wanted to come. I am not resentful, but I want to illustrate the spirit of one particular Greek priest. Because our house was convent property, the priest would occasionally cut the electricity. "I don't want this to be a Lutheran Bible study," he would announce to my father.

I don't talk about this very much, but my father's idea was that our home was not to be a house of cards and drinking, like many of the houses in the Old City, but a house of God. We, of course, didn't have television. So the weekly Bible study provided a positive alternative for whoever came. I would come home after my studies and, when I grew older, I translated for the preacher whom my father brought from the Brethren church. The idea was not to make the gathering Brethren or Lutheran, but a Bible study in an evangelical spirit. For this reason, I used to speak with my parents about my studying theology, because I felt the call when I was eleven years old.

My home life was fully supportive of me. And many people might think that it was better at that time to become a pastor for financial reasons. But my father never said this. Rather, he always said, "If you want to find better financial opportunities, they are there, but that's not the reason to be a pastor. To serve the Lord, this is the best reason."

Young Adulthood

In June 1967, we were faced with another war. My mother wondered if this might be the time when we would move back to her old neighborhood in West Jerusalem. Others were afraid that Israel wanted to expand its borders. Once again, we sought shelter in the basement of the Greek Orthodox church in our compound. One afternoon, my mother Alice had gone up to our house to fetch some food for us to eat. That's when she first heard the Israeli soldiers and she came in dancing.

"I heard voices in the street," she said. "I could recognize that they weren't speaking Arabic. For nineteen years, there have been no Jews in the Old City. Now, I heard Jewish voices."

She ran down to inform the others in the church. "Schlomo Moshe. Yehuda. Yehuda," she cried.

They all thought she was crazy, like Rhoda in the book of Acts announcing Peter's escape from prison.

"The Arab Legion will protect us," was the most common response. Yet, it was not long before they all realized that Israel had conquered the Old City.

We adjusted to the changes. My main concern at the time was to complete my education. In 1968, I sat for the *tawjihi,* the comprehensive examination that determines the future for every young Arab man and woman. I wrote a good exam, the third-best mark in the Ramallah district.

I then expressed my desire at the Lutheran church to become a pastor. The pastors all responded in the same way. "Oh, we are young, all of us," they said. "We don't need a new pastor." But they couldn't argue, because my marks were excellent and they recognized my calling. So they agreed that the probst, the head of Redeemer Church, should consult with the German church about my theological education. Likely, as they informed me, I would be trained as a missionary, perhaps to go to Tanzania.

I waited and waited, but nothing materialized. The pastors felt that it was important to keep my interest, so the probst hired me to be the church doorkeeper. This was the beginning of my work in the church. I would let people go up in the Redeemer tower. I would greet visitors. I would take messages and answer questions. I enjoyed it.

Each evening, I would watch the door in the reception area until nine o'clock. Then I would walk home alone at night in the streets. It is important to remember that this was shortly after the 1967 war. People were still living in fear and adjusting to Israeli rule. There would be nobody in the streets at night but the police and soldiers and me. I remember trembling for fear as I made my way home. What might they do if they were to catch me, a young man walking in the streets? It was only a two-minute walk, but I was really afraid. This is part of the difficult life that I lived, and, of course, I'm proud of it, because it helped me to find my Palestinian identity.

After the 1967 war, I also had my first encounter with fundamentalist Christian theology. An American Alliance pastor from West Jerusalem appeared at our door with his evangelizing message. "Thank God, that Israel has liberated the Old City," he proclaimed. He instructed us to open up our Bibles where God's will would be made clear. First, it was Daniel 7. He began reading the description of visions with four winds and four beasts coming up out of the sea. "Don't you see?" he asked. "The lion, the bear, the leopard, the fourth beast. These represent the four Arab nations: Jordan, Egypt, Syria, and Lebanon." Then he went on to interpret the ten horns as Arab countries and the one small horn as the emerging state of Israel. "Don't you see, son?" he addressed me. "The Scripture is fulfilled."

The next week this evangelical preacher returned. For some time, he continued to visit us, often bringing food and doing what he could to help our family. "Is God meddling in politics?" I wanted to know. This approach to the Bible was rather intriguing. Some of these images corresponded to popular Middle Eastern symbols. The Palestinians had always employed the image of the eagle. I was told to read about the foolish Egyptians in Isaiah 19:11-15 and the defeated Iraqis in Jeremiah 50:9, 14. It all made sense to my intellect. Yet in my heart, something was not quite right. I knew then that I wanted to study the Old Testament. I had so many questions. We were living in an atmosphere of fear. We were losers. We should be quiet. Yet faced with occupation, I needed to make theological sense of this situation. Does God allow injustice? Is God only a God of power? Is this the end for us?

I needed more in life than to be a doorkeeper. Since I didn't go to work until the afternoons, I decided to study Hebrew. Each morning I traveled to Ulpan Beit Ha'am in West Jerusalem to study Hebrew, and in the afternoons I worked at the church. I didn't give in. I was working. I knew my father could not pay it, so I paid with my church wages for my Hebrew studies, which helped me in the university and still help me now. I studied six months. I learned that my Hebrew teachers read the prophets in a way totally different from the fundamentalist pastor. Studying Hebrew began to raise in my mind theological questions about the Old Testament, about the Jews, and about the land. How did all that fit together? My interest in the Old Testament grew. It is not surprising that I would eventually write my dissertation on election in Isaiah 40–55, known as Deutero-Isaiah.

All along, I had in the back of my mind that I would be going abroad to further my education. Perhaps after a certain length of time, it is true, I wanted to find a way out of the occupation. An outlet—what do you call it in psychology?—a kind of escapism. You cannot bear it. Everything is closed. Everything is blocked, unclear. You are powerless. That is what life was like for Palestinians, including myself. But I would never give in to frustration and despair. Truly, my living faith through my childhood already helped me to meet these challenges and not to give up. It is a faith based on hardships, not a faith based on luxury.

Study in Finland

After nine months, my application for a scholarship to Germany was not successful. I had always assumed that I would go to Germany, because I thought there was no other option to study theology. Then, something happened that would change my life. I know about April 20, 1969—I remember it very well—my mother came home to tell me, "Munib, I think we have to send you to Finland to study diaconia."

I thought, "Finland? Where is Finland? A cold country—I'll never go there." And the second disappointment—I was to study for the diaconate, not theology for the pastorate. "For heaven's sake, are you killing my future?" I was always asking, never submitting. "You are killing my future." I was always debating with my parents, but never rude.

My parents responded in a very practical way. They said, "Okay, if you wait to go to Germany, maybe you will not get a scholarship, and you will stay here. The longer you stay, the harder it will be for you. You are now young. You can easily grasp things. The older you become, the more difficult it will be. Study diaconia. If you are good, you will study theology. If you are not successful, you will remain as you are. Why do you take the tenth step before taking the first step?"

They tried to persuade me that the place of study did not matter so much. They said, "The people in Finland, as far as we know, are good people. What is the difference between Finland and those other cold countries? Maybe you know a little bit of German, and you think it will be easier for you. But what is the difference?"

So I told them, "Let me think." My parents were open, not compelling me. I felt cornered. I didn't know if I was right or not. After a while, I said, "Okay."

My mother then announced, "The probst will introduce you this evening to two gentlemen from Finland."

I said, "What for?" and wondered what had been taking place. Nevertheless, that same evening, I went to the church office to meet the probst. There I was, eighteen and a half years old. I used to be a bit timid, working at the reception area and seeing important visitors come and go. Because we were in the Jordanian era, we were educated to show high respect for all authority.

So these two Finnish men, one a pastor, the other a deacon, asked, "Do you know why we are here?" I said, "Please explain."

They answered, "There is a pastor in Finland who is in charge of a school of diaconia in Järvenpää, forty miles north of Helsinki. For the celebration of his fiftieth birthday, friends collected money with the goal of bringing somebody to study diaconia, either from South Africa or from Palestine. We thought South Africa was too far, so we came here to find somebody. We are here to choose a Palestinian to study diaconia."

I didn't know what to say. How can you answer? Instead of asking, "What do you think?" they asked, "Are you ready to come?" This was the question. Not, "Do you think you will come?" or "Do you think this is a good idea?" They were answering the question for me. "If you are ready to come, we think in one month's time you will be in Finland."

The probst had been standing quietly by, but now he addressed me, "I think it's a good offer." This was Probst Hansjörg Köhler, who is still living and remains a good friend. "I think it's a good offer," he repeated. "Why should you stay here?"

I countered that I had wanted to study theology. He gave the same argument that my mother gave. On April 26, I received the official letter offering the scholarship, and they told me, "We will wait one week for your decision." They added, "We like you and think that you will do well in school."

I asked, "How? Why?" How did they know me? It was God's plan. Later, of course, I would come to know well both these men and the pastor responsible for the scholarship, Pastor Simo Palosuo, a leading theologian in Finland, working in cooperation with the Association of Deacons in Finland, and the Finnish Evangelical Lutheran Mission. A few years ago when he passed away, I wrote a letter to be read at his funeral. Even his family, except for his wife, were unaware of what he had done, bringing a young Palestinian to study in Finland.

In six weeks, I got my laissez-passer, my Israeli travel documents, which was nearly impossible at that time and renewed annually. I got my visa for Finland in one day and my tickets in four. By June 5, 1969, I was in Finland alone in an empty mission house to study Finnish and to prepare myself in three months to enter the college to study diaconia. They picked a fine teacher for me. I never regretted it later. But when you are young and don't know things, it is different. I had a lot of misgivings, but what other choice did I have? I accepted that this was part of God's way in calling me for ministry.

So I studied diaconia for three years. Unfortunately, or fortunately, it was too easy for me and the teachers knew it, even though it was in Finnish. They would ask me, "Did you previously study theology?" I said, "No." They said, "You know more than we do. How?"

My education in the Lutheran schools had been so deep that I grasped all the major points. I believe that I could have been a teacher of Christian education, even at that time. For example, we were required to know the three missionary journeys of Paul, even with the details about every single town along the way—Lystra, Derbe, and so on. The Lutheran schools really played a good role in molding my identity. Always in education, we find teachers we don't like, teachers who are tough, but we remember those teachers who really took us in their hands. My Lutheran education was not a wishy-washy enterprise that would have made me shaky or afraid of circumstances, but it molded my character, strong and confident.

During my third year of diaconia studies, I started some minor courses in theology. Soon, I finished my diaconate, and immediately I wrote to my church that I wanted to continue to study theology. They gave me the okay.

That meant that my laissez-passer had to be renewed. The school director contacted the Israeli ambassador to inform him that I would be coming. Still, it was a terrifying moment for me. Even after one year away from Jerusalem, the experience of Israeli occupation affected me. I remember standing on the street before the Israeli Embassy when my body started shaking uncontrollably. I offered a prayer. At the first door, my identity was checked, and I was searched. I was informed that the laissez-passer was normally issued in Israel.

Nevertheless, an official agreed to see me. He was Michael Ben Yehuda, first secretary of the Israeli Embassy. As I sat in his office, he surprised me with his willingness to help. "Young man," he said, "I want to help you because you are a Christian."

"Thank you," I politely responded.

"No, you do not need to thank me," he offered. "In Italy, members of the Catholic church hid me and saved my life. If it were not for the Christians, I would not be here. I am happy to help."

It was important for me to hear his message. There was none of the bitter tone that often had characterized Israelis I had encountered in Jerusalem before I left home.

Later Mr. Ben Yehuda offered me encouragement. "I don't want you to become a deacon, but a pastor," he told me. "I will talk with your teachers."

What a change from the fear I had felt before entering the embassy. I realized that my dream might become a reality.

The last thing he told me left an imprint on my memory. "I want to attend your ordination," he said. "Please let me know, and I will come."

As it turned out, however, he did not attend my ordination. By that time in 1976, I had learned that he was working in the Foreign Ministry in Jerusalem. So I took a letter to his office inviting him to this event, but he did not attend. I soon forgot about him and his words of encouragement. Not until two decades later were our paths to cross. In 1993, when the archbishop of Finland, John Vikström, came to Jerusalem, I was invited to a reception at the Finnish Embassy in Tel Aviv. There, the chairperson of the Finnish Israel Society was introduced as Michael Ben Yehuda.

He looked at me uncertainly. He asked if I knew someone who had studied theology with the name Younan. I said, "It is I." "Yes, I remember," he said giving me a hug. "I am fulfilled. I played a role."

Thanks to his help and that of many others, my time in Finland was successful. In seven years, I received both bachelor's and master's degrees.

Finland helped to shape my national identity as a Palestinian. Some said, "Get your Ph.D." I said, "No, I am called to serve my people. I can get my Ph.D. later on." People might argue with me that I was mistaken.

I had also been engaged with Palestinian politics for the first time in Finland. German missionaries used to tell us that, if you are in the church, you should have nothing to do with politics. So, when I was interested in politics, I thought I was not a good Christian. Yet, in Finland, I often visited a congregation in the evening. The first thing they would do was raise the Finnish flag and sing the national anthem. Then, they had a prayer and Bible reading. What is this, nationalism? Why with the Germans was I not allowed to be nationalistic? This was boiling in my heart. Whenever I spoke of politics, I was afraid I was committing a sin, because of my evangelical background. So I would feel guilty. But the archbishop of Finland began speaking about the "motherland" and about their pride in 1917 and 1942 when they won independence from the Russians. It was a shock, a cultural shock and a theological shock. I could not raise my flag. At this time in 1970–72, the Palestine Liberation Organization (PLO) was very active, and everybody thought Palestinians were terrorists as they do now, or even worse. There was no communication with America or with Israel. I thought, Why?

There were maybe fifty foreigners in Finland, and we knew each other. The other Arab expatriates would say, "Come, we will go drink some beer and talk politics." I would say, "No, no, no." I was so afraid. Speaking of politics was a sin, because of my upbringing. So it took time, maybe one to two years before I began to feel I was a Palestinian Christian. I began to climb the mountain of constructive nationalism.

When I speak of nationalism, I mean in a positive, not in a negative, way. First of all, I'm a Christian. So what is Christian? I'm Arab. Yet, it is not enough simply to be lumped together with those from other Arab countries. I'm a Palestinian. That's distinctive. The more I climbed the nationalist mountain, the more I was conscious of my Christian identity. The more that I was conscious of my Christian identity, the more I became conscious of my Palestinian identity. They grew along parallel tracks, increasing to the same degree. Had I not been in Finland, would I have gained that identity?

The Finnish Christians would always say, "You're from Jerusalem. Let us put the Israeli flag up for you. Shall we play for you the national anthem of Israel?" They made the analogy that they had won against the Russians, and Israel had won against the Arabs.

All of this aroused my own nationalism. At first, I politely accepted, but I never felt comfortable. The Israeli flag and national anthem did not represent me, a Palestinian Christian. So I became more aware of the issue in my studies. I tried to see what is political, what is human, what is divine. What is God's plan, and what is other? Reading Luther at that time in school, I was impressed with one hermeneutical principle, *Was Christus treibet?* What carries Christ? I began to see clearly that I could be Christian and Palestinian at the same time.

This development was also related to a new appreciation for contextual theology. I came to understand that Finnish theology had been influenced by their own revival movements. The gospel had been adapted to the Finnish environment through effective lay preachers. Their style was unique with home gatherings and preachers sitting in rocking chairs, who leisurely prolonged their messages over the course of several hours. There is no question that this method would never work in a Palestinian context. Yet this was the point. The question was not so much about methodology, but about why people were interested. Somehow, these lay preachers had touched the nerve and context of Finnish strength. They had come to understand *martyria* in the Finnish context. I came to realize the importance of a Palestinian contextualization of the gospel.

Finally, I was impressed with the universalism of Deutero-Isaiah. My dissertation was an answer to those many questions that had earlier plagued me. God was not only for one nation, but for all. There was a difference between theological Israel and the fundamentalists' political Israel. God chooses people to forward God's mission, not to glorify the nation.

I feel confident that all these factors played a role in molding my identity. I feel no regret about any of that.

By the time I finished my studies, I was not only equipped to be a pastor, I also understood my identity as a Palestinian Christian. I had traveled to the ends of the earth, where I learned to be a witness in Jerusalem.

Part II

Martyria and Nonviolence

3

A Theology of *Martyria*

Shortly after the outbreak of the al-Aqsa Intifada, sixty-year-old Harold Fisher was killed by an Israeli helicopter gunship in his town of Beit Jala. It was a gruesome death. His body was literally blown apart, limb severed from limb. He was an innocent victim of violence if ever there was one. A German doctor who had come to Beit Jala to help the Palestinian people, he had married, had children, and actively participated for over twenty years in community life, being a member at the Lutheran Church of the Reformation in Beit Jala.

While Israel was inflicting nightly helicopter raids and tank shelling on this town just south of Jerusalem, Fisher continued to treat the wounded. On the night of November 15, 2000, there was shelling and there were screams. He and his family had sought cover in their own house. Neighbors came knocking on his door for help. Yet at the cry of human need, Dr. Fisher grabbed his medical bag and ran out into the night, thinking nothing of his own safety. From the vantage of the helicopter flying overhead, there was nothing that distinguished him as a good person, as a Christian, as a doctor, as someone who could be considered an expatriate. He was a human being doing what he always did best—helping other people—and he fell victim to the violence of modern weaponry.

The next day was the funeral. It was one of the most difficult speeches I have had to give. His widow was there, and his children. Friends and community leaders. Clergy. All of a sudden we all felt very vulnerable. If death so easily takes someone like Harold Fisher, what about the rest of us, a tiny Christian community?

In my eulogy, I referred to Harold Fisher as a martyr for peace—
martys, the Greek word translated "witness." I thought nothing of it. He
had been a witness to us. He had been a witness to the whole community. In death, he was serving as a witness to the whole world.

"The Lutheran church offers a martyr who has given his life for the
service of Palestinians," I said. "We ask today: What is his guilt that he
went to give first aid to save humanity and keep the dignity of his
medical profession? What is his guilt as he came to serve the human
being, whether Palestinian or German or other, whether Christian or
Muslim? For this reason, Harry, you join today the cloud of martyrs
who gave their lives for the freedom of humanity."

Immediately afterward, several reporters gathered around looking
for their story. "Bishop, did I hear you right?" one asked. "You called
Dr. Fisher a martyr?"

"Yes."

"Isn't martyr a Muslim term for the dead? Don't you have to die
fighting to be a martyr?" They began to bombard me with questions.[1]

In our grieving, we were forced to deal with such questions. "Dr.
Fisher's whole life was a witness," I replied. "That's why I called him a
martyr."

I was once again reminded that the church needs a theology of
martyria. It's a concept misunderstood, misused, and even missing from
the vocabularies of many Christians. What does it mean to be a martyr? In a simple sense, it means no more than to be a witness. That's
how it is translated. It means a life of witnessing in word, and also in
deed. That's why someone like Harold Fisher was such a good witness.
His whole life expressed his faith—his calling as a doctor, his constant
love and care for those in need, his attitude of humble service. Dr. Fisher
did not hesitate to speak of his faith, but what is more important, he
lived it. So he witnessed in word and in deed. The third component is
suffering. *Martyria* is expressed when one's faith makes one vulnerable
to the suffering of this world. It means exposing oneself, risking one's
life for the other, as did Dr. Fisher when he went out from the safety of
his home that November night. That's what it means to be a martyr.

Challenges

"You will be my witnesses in Jerusalem, in all Judea and Samaria, and
to the ends of the earth." These were the last words spoken by Jesus to

his disciples in Acts 1:8. When I read these words today, there are three fundamental problems in understanding them—each connected with religious fundamentalism: Jewish, Muslim, and Christian.

When I read this text in my congregations, my people stumble over the phrase "in all Judea and Samaria" because these terms are applied to the Palestinian West Bank territory by Jewish fundamentalists who claim a right to the land because they say the Bible tells them so. The modern use of this phrase, popularized by former Prime Minister Menachem Begin, has been renewed by current Prime Minister Ariel Sharon. For them, the terminology is not the West Bank or the Occupied Territories, but Judea and Samaria—the land God gave the Jews. It carries with it a glorification of the settler—like Baruch Goldstein who was declared *tsaddiq,* "righteous," for his role in carrying out the Hebron massacre at the Tomb of the Patriarchs. Does witness address political issues? Indeed, it does. Yet it is a call for justice and human dignity—concepts that will be addressed throughout this book.

A second problem comes from Christian fundamentalists who want to place all the focus on the oral proclamation. Witness for them is defined as evangelism and passing out tracts. The modern evangelical movement—in contrast to the historic churches of the Reformation—has placed all the emphasis on the verbal witness. The contemporary world, too, attempts to forget that linkage of word and deed. A passive witness is enough. One is free to have one's opinions, but don't go to the extreme. Believe them, but don't carry them out in daily life. Witness has too often been separated from the deed, separated from the risk of suffering. This is a far cry from the witness described in the Acts of the Apostles, a witness defined as word and deed, a witness to the whole person and by the whole person, a witness that encompasses all of life.

The third problem comes from Muslim fundamentalists who tie martyrdom to death—often violent death while fighting for their cause. This kind of *martyria* has been thrust to the forefront by suicide bomb attacks carried out in the name of religion and with the expectation of rewards in paradise. Such an understanding of *ashada* (martyrdom) has been challenged by the mainstream of Islam during the months following the September 11 suicide attacks on the World Trade Center. Likewise, as H. Strathmann, writing on the New Testament concept of *martyria,* notes, "Stephen is not called a witness because he dies; he dies because he is a witness of Christ."[2] Witness is not just about death, it is about life. It is about living fully in such a way that death is the outcome.

The Acts of the Apostles

The concept of *martyria* is essential to the story of the earliest Christians in the Acts of the Apostles. At the beginning, Jesus commissions the disciples, "You will be my witnesses in Jerusalem ... and to the ends of the earth" (Acts 1:8). It reaches full form in the stories of the struggles of those following the Way as they stand before hostile authorities (Acts 2:32; 3:15; 5:32; 10:39, 41). It reaches fulfillment with the story of Paul crossing the northern Mediterranean world to reach Rome as the notorious Nero begins to lift his threatening hand for the worst persecution the early church was to know. From the beginning, from that earth-shattering experience on the Damascus road (Acts 26:16) and from his deathbed, where he received healing and baptism from Ananias (Acts 22:15), Paul was fully aware that his witness would only expose him to suffering.

The impact of this phenomenon of Christian risk-filled witness in the early church was so dramatic that the Greek word *martyria* was imbedded in the language of the church. We have "the age of martyrs" and a whole genre of literature called martyrologies. In the English language, the word *martyr* does not have to be explained. A martyr is someone who dies for his or her faith.

Witness in the Old Testament

In the Old Testament, the closest equivalent to *martyria* is the Hebrew term *'ed* or *'edah* (over one hundred times). This is the term used when testimony is given in court, where a person is expected to speak truthfully about what he or she has experienced.[3] Yet this is a long way from the risk-taking element in the Acts of the Apostles.

We are reminded that the message cannot be separated from the person. The Old Testament provides its share of forerunners for the New Testament martyrs. The character Daniel immediately comes to mind. He witnesses by worshiping God, and the consequence of his actions is suffering. Jonah is a story of practical *martyria*. His refusal to hear, his attempted escape from his calling, his rejection—all lead to suffering, which in this case comes from the very hand of God. It demonstrates how sometimes people are witnesses without even being aware of it.

The prophets would all fit the criteria of *martyria*. Jeremiah, certainly, was a living witness in all he said and did, yet he was never accepted during his lifetime. He endured rejection and suffering. The same can be said for Amos and Micah. In a very strange way Hosea, in following God's command to marry a prostitute, became a witness before God, before his wife, before Israel, who were all the time mocking him. His suffering was in his shame. A prophet's witness was never hidden or compromised. It was always evident to the world. "Is it you, you troubler of Israel?"—so Ahab addressed Elijah (1 Kings 18:17)—or "Have you found me, my enemy?" (1 Kings 21:20). Even in a foreign country his witness was known, "I know that you are a man of God, and that the word of the LORD in your mouth is true" (1 Kings 17:24).

Deutero-Isaiah gives a model for the New Testament witness.[4] Isaiah 43–44 is an intriguing section because God arranges a kind of trial in the presence of all the nations to show who truly is God. Three times Israel is told: "You are my witnesses"[5] (Isaiah 43:10, 12; 44:8). Interestingly, the witness is also identified with the "Servant of God," interpreted by the early church as a reference to Jesus. "You are my witnesses, says the LORD, and my servant whom I have chosen, so that you may know and believe me and understand that I am he" (Isaiah 43:10). In chapter 53, this figure's role is clearly one of suffering. Likewise, this is implicit in the case of the witnesses. "Do not fear, or be afraid," God offers reassurance (Isaiah 44:8).

For our small Palestinian community, the words occurring at the beginning of Isaiah 43 are a constant source of comfort and strength:

> Do not fear, for I have redeemed you;
>   I have called you by name, you are mine.
> When you pass through the waters, I will be with you;
>   and through the rivers, they shall not overwhelm you;
> when you walk through fire you shall not be burned,
>   and the flame shall not consume you. (Isaiah 43:1-2)

Christ as Model of Witness

Because of the reference to the servant who suffers for his witness, one cannot help but focus on the death of Jesus. The term *martys* or *martyrion* is strangely never used for Christ in this sense in the Gospels, but there we see clearly what it means to be a witness. As soon as Jesus begins his ministry of preaching and healing in Galilee, the reader is told, "The Pharisees went out and immediately conspired with the Herodians against him, how to destroy him" (Mark 3:6). Later, when he realizes the inevitability of his journey to Jerusalem, Jesus speaks the three passion predictions to his disciples. "The Son of Man must undergo great suffering and be rejected by the elders, and the chief priests, and the scribes, and be killed, and after three days rise again" (Mark 8:31; 9:31; 10:33-34). Yet he does not shy away from the witness he must make in Jerusalem. "Jerusalem, Jerusalem, the city that kills the prophets and stones those who are sent to it!" (Luke 13:34). With these words, he sets his face toward Jerusalem. He hesitates before neither the chief priests nor the Roman governor Pilate, accepting his fate of crucifixion. In death, there is no ambiguity about his witness. In response, the centurion pronounces his confession, "Truly this man was God's Son!" (Mark 15:39). Nowhere else do the three components of witness come together so well as in the ministry of Christ: witnessing in word, witnessing in deed, and exposing oneself to danger, whatever the cost.

In every aspect of living, a person is a witness. As is commonly attributed to St. Francis of Assisi, "Go out and preach the Gospel. If necessary, use words." *Martyria* is witness in both word and deed. In the character of Paul, one sees a model for the Christian of one who carries in his own flesh the suffering of Christ.

In the Acts of the Apostles, Stephen was the witness par excellence (Acts 6–7; 22:20). He did not divide what he said from what he did. He received his commission from the early church for diaconia, to provide a ministry of service. Yet service was no more important than his words, just as words were no more important than the deeds of the early apostles. Both meant taking up the cross and following the Lord. Stephen clearly illustrates that there can be joy in suffering. Yet it cannot be suffering simply for the sake of suffering. Joy in suffering comes to a victim of injustice.

That kind of joy illuminates the martyrdom of Polycarp—the second-century bishop of Smyrna who took his witness to the seat of power in Rome. "For eighty-six years, I have been his servant, and God has never done me wrong," he said. "How can I blaspheme my king who saved me?"

"I have wild beasts," announced the government official. "I shall throw you to them, if you don't change your attitude."

"Call them," replied the old man. "We cannot change our attitude if it means a change from better to worse. But it is a splendid thing to change from cruelty to justice."

The threats changed from wild beasts to fire. When the pyre was ready, Polycarp prayed: "I bless you for counting me worthy of this day and hour, that in the number of martyrs I may partake of Christ's cup, to the resurrection of eternal life."[6]

Witness As a Minority

Martyria seems to have had a close connection with the minority status of early Christians. That kind of witness must be distinguished from much of the mission work of the church today, whose proclamation of the gospel comes from a majority point of view.

This is significant for the Palestinian Christian. At a time when Christians comprise less than 2 percent of the Palestinian population and 5 percent in the entire Arab world, we are very mindful of our minority status. In some parts of the world, the majority status of Christianity is significant. People become Christian simply because it is the popular thing to do.

Here, it is a constant effort to continue the Christian witness. It would be easier to emigrate. It would be easier to convert. It would be easier to secularize. Yet, being a minority itself is a witness. When you are such a small minority, you stand out. People know who you are. You are a witness whatever you do. Even if a Christian never proclaims the word of God, one's whole being may speak loudly the message of Christ's love. Sometimes, it is the simple act of love in dealing with a neighbor, or with someone of another religion, or even with an enemy. Being a minority means being exposed. That's why it is witness in word and deed together; it is witness that exposes one to possible suffering. There is no cheap martyr. Witnessing from such a minority status carries a price.

Freedom of religion is something taken for granted in parts of the world. It is not the case everywhere. What about those living in countries where mission laws exist? What about societies where the only opportunity to climb the ladder of success through positions in government or in the community is completely dependent upon one's religion? The call of Christ to take up the cross and follow carries with it the component of self-denial and the risk of losing one's life. Jesus made this clear when the sons of Zebedee requested to sit at his right and left hand in the kingdom (Mark 10:34-45). Instead, servanthood is held up as the model of discipleship. Here is a stark difference between Christian *martyria* and the Jewish and Muslim views of martyrdom as carried out for the martyr's own benefit. Jesus responds that James and John will drink the cup, whatever the will of God might be for their future honor. As Thomas à Kempis said, "Many are breaking bread, but few are drinking the cup."[7] It is our calling to drink the cup.

Witness As Living

The true witness does not dwell on the suffering. In some cases, it has become a fact of life that only an outside observer recognizes. One simply lives life fully as if Christ were living in one.

Once as I was walking through the Old City, several Muslim friends called out to me. "You Christians are better than we Muslims," they remarked. There was no sarcasm or poking fun in their remarks. They were completely sincere. They had been observing a woman known to be a Christian, and they began talking among themselves. "Look at her, how she carries that disabled child and cares for him! Each day she passes by, never complaining. And it's not even her own child."

"This is what Christ teaches," I simply said.

That woman was a witness. She was likely unaware that she was even being observed.

Experiences like that make me conscious of my own daily walk through life. I am observed every day—observed in a positive sense, not for criticism. I need to be serious about my own witness.

Another day, I was in conversation with a Jewish friend. He remarked, "You Christians have taught me much about forgiveness."

"But I don't think we have ever really had a discussion on the subject of forgiveness," I offered a mild protest.

"You have taught me through everyday living," he responded. "For Jews, if we sin, then punishment and an act of atonement must follow. For Muslims, there must be atonement and then consulting the *shariah*. For Christians, however, you teach how to be forgiven even if you sin."

"It is not because we Christians are good," I replied, "but because Jesus died for our sins. That brings forgiveness."

"And we have come to understand that from our regular inter-action with you."

These are simple illustrations, but they show how our witness in word and deed cannot be separated in this context.

I am often called upon to give commencement speeches, which, of course, address mixed audiences of Muslims and Christians. Often, I have thought that I am not saying anything new or different. Yet Muslim parents come up to me afterward expressing appreciation. It is more than the common polite comments. "You have touched our hearts," they have told me on more than one occasion.

So what was unique about my talk? As I think about it, there must be something of that constant effort to balance law and gospel in my words. There is the constant assumption of a theology of grace, show-ing that I am moving about in God's hands, not that God is controlled by our hands. My witness is molded through the theology of the cross, that we are called not to be masters, but servants.

Most of the time, I am simply unaware of my role as a witness. Once I am aware, then there is the danger of projecting myself. Once I am proud, I am no longer a witness. It is the recognition of these em-phases that helps us to understand that our witness in word and deed exposes us to suffering.

Witness for Justice

If I am called to suffering, I need to accept it as God's will. When we look at the witnessing life of Jesus, we see that he clearly understood the inevitability of the cross ahead. Gethsemane provides that dramatic setting where he was confronted with that reality and where he accepted the cup. As we observe Jesus on the cross, one message is obvious: do not be blindly submissive to our own theologies.

A simplistic view might say, "I'm called to suffer. That elevates me." God calls us to *martyria,* but not to accept the evil that causes suffering. *Martyria* still carries with it a kind of dignity, the same way Jesus' dignity remained intact on the cross.

Perhaps our understanding of suffering can be clarified through Luther's idea of *simul justus et peccator.* A Christian is at the same time both saint and sinner. A person does not dwell on the sin but works to overcome it. One who witnesses carries a certain dignity, yet is called to suffer. We need to beware of theologies of glory. It would be a sin for a seriously sick person not to go to the doctor. How absurd it would be for them to ignore the causes of their illness and to raise up their suffering as a sign of God's glory.

In our context, we must address the issue of suffering injustice. God simply does not will injustice. Everything about God in the biblical record points to a clear condemnation of injustice. To suffer injustice calls one to work against injustice.

There is always the danger of a victim mentality. Perhaps being a victim has the appeal of being also the recipient of compassion. Playing the victim also can put one in a position of power as others around you are manipulated. But it plays on the powerful emotions of guilt and does not want to let go. The danger is that the victim becomes the oppressor. This kind of individual must always have an ex-enemy to survive. Holding on to resentment, one eventually becomes one's own enemy.

Nelson Mandela never allowed his suffering to create a bondage of victimization. When he was released from prison in South Africa, the first person he went to meet was the one who imprisoned him. He had to get over the past. As a result, his dignity was restored. *Martyria* is neither victimization nor does it play on guilt. The most important of Jesus' words from the cross are "Father, forgive them" (Luke 23:34). Through this forgiveness, there is liberation, and it is through liberation that one finds dignity, even in suffering.

This is why it was crucial for Pope John Paul II during the Jubilee pilgrimage to make his major mea culpa at Yad Vashem—the Jerusalem Holocaust memorial. He apologized for the mistakes of those in the church who persecuted the Jewish people. In so doing, he brought forgiveness so that all can be liberated from the past, lest the Holocaust should be repeated again against the Jewish people or against any nation.

While the Palestinian people can easily be persuaded to dwell on the past, their strength is that they are not living in a mentality of fear. They are empowered because they believe that truth and justice are on their side. The Intifada may not make any sense from a logical standpoint. What hope is there for an uprising against the region's strongest army? What hope is there for children throwing stones against powerful tanks and weaponry? The Intifada has not arisen out of a desire to call attention to the people's suffering or to play the victim. It comes rather from a sense of empowerment. That in itself is a witness.

In Weakness I Am Strong

It has often been said that the church in Palestine is walking its own Via Dolorosa. The church in Palestine is small. It is fragmented and its organization is different from the West. There are thirteen churches in the one-square-kilometer area called the Old City of Jerusalem. There is constant attention to historic *Status Quo* agreements and constant maneuvering with respect to protocol. In many ways, this is the weakest church in the world—financially, structurally, even numerically. As Lutherans, we are only a small part of the Jerusalem church. I could easily paraphrase Paul to say that I am least of all the bishops, not worthy to be called a bishop. We are that small.

The paradox is that, in spite of weakness, we are a formidable witness. As Paul said, "My power is made perfect in weakness" (2 Corinthians 12:9). Or again, "We have this treasure in clay jars" (2 Corinthians 4:7). We are frail. We are weak. But the message makes our weak body stronger.

Why did God put me here? This is a question every Palestinian must ask. All the time when I was studying in Finland, I always felt God's strings pulling me home. Every time I am away in another country at a conference or attending meetings, even in those relatively free and relaxing environments, I feel the need to get back to Jerusalem with all its tensions, frustrations, and difficulties.

Logically, there is no future here. Our numbers continue to dwindle. The prolonged occupation increases the obstacles to carrying out our ministry. Official Israeli attitudes toward the church are increasingly hostile. The lure of emigration for Christians is especially attractive since they have family connections elsewhere, since many have high educational degrees, and since their economic potential is much better anywhere else but here. Why should we stay, against our logical interests?

Witness to the Resurrection

Yet, there is a spiritual future. That is what *martyria* is all about. The Palestinian church is not called to a life of ease, comfort, and luxury. It is called to be a witness in word and deed, exposing itself to suffering. The Palestinian church is called to take up its cross and to follow the Way of Jesus. *Martyria* is the Via Dolorosa with resurrection.

This takes us back to the Acts of the Apostles. It is significant that the disciples were not called witnesses until after the resurrection. In Luke's gospel, it is only at the very end—following the account of the passion, death, and resurrection—that the risen Jesus commissions the disciples to be witnesses, instructing them to wait in Jerusalem for the empowering of the Holy Spirit (Luke 24:48). These words are repeated almost verbatim in the context of a resurrection appearance in Acts 1:8. So what is the heart of their testimony? "This Jesus God raised up, and of that all of us are witnesses" (Acts 2:32; see also 3:15; 5:32). *Martyria* is not so much about death as it is about life. This is what empowers our church.

The Lutheran Church of the Redeemer: A Place for Witness

We are fortunate as Lutherans to have magnificent facilities in the heart of the Old City of Jerusalem. Our bell tower provides a spectacular vantage point from which to view the entire city: the four Quarters of the Old City, the domed roofs of churches, the minarets of mosques, and the modern plaza of the Western Wall complex. At the same time, that white limestone bell tower is visible throughout the city. Tour guides standing with their groups at the Mount of Olives lookout often use it as a marker to point visitors to surrounding sites such as the Church of the Holy Sepulchre or David's tower.

"How are you so fortunate to have a church in such a prominent location?" many tourists ask.

The land was a gift from the Turkish sultan to the Prussian king in 1869. In turn, Kaiser Wilhelm II ordered in 1893 that a church be built for the local community. He, in fact, attended the dedication of the impressive sanctuary and of the entire church complex five years later.

Our location can be seen in terms of good fortune. It is also a reminder of our responsibility to be witnesses in the midst of this bustling city. Just to our south, the Jewish Quarter begins. To the west is the Armenian Quarter; to the north, the Christian Quarter; to the east, the Muslim Quarter. All around us are various churches, mosques, and synagogues. Our responsibility is to be a living witness in this diverse community.

Our location also reminds us of our heritage of word and service. The immediate area surrounding the church is called the Muristan, derived from the Persian word for hospital or hospice. From as early as the ninth century, there are records of pilgrims finding a place of refuge here. Then, during a time of great suffering and conflict for our city—the time known in the West as the Crusades—this was the location where a group of knights chose to provide healing rather than destruction. The Knights of St. John of the Hospital erected a building for the wounded and weak and provided a safe haven for visitors. This remains our witness nearly a millennium later.

There is one more layer of history to this place. It is so difficult for modern visitors to imagine the layout of walls and buildings of the Roman-era city. The present city wall was erected only five hundred years ago. One needs to strip away in his or her mind all of these later structures. Two thousand years ago, the north wall of the city passed underneath what would become our sanctuary. There were no houses, no bustling streets, no Church of the Holy Sepulchre—only a rock quarry was outside the city walls. Here, on an outcropping known as Golgotha, was the site for Roman executions.

From the front door of the Lutheran Church of the Redeemer, it is only a stone's throw to the site of the historic church built by Constantine. It is only a matter of meters from our church to the site of Golgotha. There is an old tradition that the place where the women stood watching on that Friday noon is none other than the ground beneath our church complex. Out of the way from immediate contact with hostile soldiers, yet close enough to keep watch carefully, Mary Magdalene, Mary the mother of Jesus, Joanna, Susanna, and the other women stood by quietly.

They are mentioned by name three different times within a short segment of the gospel tradition. They watch the crucifixion. They observe closely the burial nearby. They return Sunday morning to see an empty tomb and a risen Jesus. The women are the first witnesses. They go and tell. They live out their calling in word and deed. They expose themselves to suffering.

What does this mean for us as a church in the heart of the Old City? Perhaps some would suggest that we should construct a memorial where we could call attention to ourselves and bring in lots of money. That, of course, would be missing the point. Our location is a reminder of our calling to be witnesses, beginning here in Jerusalem and continuing to the ends of the earth. From our vantage point, we are in constant view of the Church of the Holy Sepulchre. From our vantage point, everything we see is through the lens of the cross and the resurrection. The women at the tomb become an example for us. They teach us the way of *martyria*.

4

Witness in the Land

When Jesus said, "You will be witnesses," that commission was linked to the land.[1] "You will be witnesses in Jerusalem, in all Judea and Samaria" (Acts 1:8). My calling is to be a witness in Jerusalem. I cannot escape it. This is my heritage. This is my life. Yet the land of my birth is a source of conflict.

Some of the root conflicts in the Middle East may be traced to the erroneous interpretation of the divine promise made some four thousand years ago, to give Palestine to Abraham and to his seed as an everlasting possession.

The issue of land is the major issue in the Palestinian–Israeli conflict. A number of years ago, Colin Chapman wrote a book, the title of which, *Whose Promised Land?*,[2] asked whether the land is for Palestinians or Israelis? Is it for Jews, Christians, or Muslims? Chapman did not have an easy definitive answer, but he was able to address the complexity of the issue. What is more important, he was able to demonstrate that the question must be addressed with careful historical critical analysis. It no longer will do, as some fundamentalists desire, to accept the ancient statements at face value.

The issue of land has dominated theological discussions on the Middle East since 1948. Is the promise of God pertaining to the land everlasting? Is God a real estate broker? Is God just or one-sided? All these questions have given rise to a very serious crisis in the life of the Palestinian Christians, driving some to the point of leaving the church. For this very reason, the church should not be quiet!

I believe that we need to be even more immersed in the land than ever. That is, the church should promote more studies in the deeper understanding of the land among Palestinian Christians. The church has to present a sound theology of the land to confront superficial and simplistic readings of the ancient texts.

The Land is a Gift from God

The story of the land starts from the covenant between God and Abraham. "I am the Lord who brought you from Ur of the Chaldeans to give you this land to possess" (Genesis 15:7). This is an expression repeated several times in the Pentateuch. The first lesson is that the land did not belong to Abraham or to the Hebrews or to their ancestors from the beginning of the time. Nobody can claim that they owned it from time immemorial. The promise came to them at that particular time as a gift from God. They did nothing to deserve it, nor did they acquire it through their own cleverness or skill in war. God says very clearly and simply: "... the land is mine; with me you are but aliens and tenants" (Leviticus 25:23).

The Palestinians, who have lived in the land and who understand how its character changes with political transitions have been among the first to recognize the land as gift. Among them is Latin Patriarch Michel Sabbah, who writes, "The promises are part of the Covenant, and the first promises dealt with temporal realities (land, kingdom, etc....)."[3] He notes that land is a sign of God's incredible generosity, exhibited in rather concrete ways.

The concept of the land as a promise has evolved according to the different life experiences of the chosen people. From the time of Abraham, the land was closely bound to the practices of nomadic tribes who divided up the lands that they occupied during the wanderings (Genesis 12:4-6). During this period, the land was understood to be a gift of God and a sign of blessing. God spoke to Abram, "All the land that you see I will give to you and to your offspring forever" (Genesis 13:15). Likewise, "I will make of you a great nation, and I will bless you, and make your name great, so that you will be a blessing" (Genesis 12:2).

As the land was a gift and a covenant promise, there were responsibilities for land tenure. It carried with it broad regulations for living in the land. There was a clear interdependence between moral behavior and land. Obedience to Yahweh was fitting in the land, and disregard of Yahweh's instruction defiled the land. Continued occupancy of the land is conditioned by faithful adherence to the admonitions. Motivation for observance of the law included the promise of continued residence. "This entire commandment that I command you today, you must diligently observe, so that you may live and increase, and go in and occupy the land" (Deuteronomy 8:1). Obedience to the ordinances would bring blessings, which, as the catalog of blessings indicates, were primarily prosperity and fruitfulness in the land (Deuteronomy 28:1-4). Israel was warned that unless it kept the statutes and the ordinances, the land would vomit up the people in it (Leviticus 18:26-28).

Two important regulations from the Old Testament dealt with land use: sabbath and jubilee. From Mount Sinai Moses issued this instruction: "When you enter the land that I am giving you, the land shall observe a sabbath to the Lord" (Leviticus 25:2). The sabbath was not something just for people but also for the land. The land was to be left fallow every seventh year in order to benefit the poor. All who were in need, the poor and alien, were to have free access to the fruits of the land. The same was to be true for the nonhuman inhabitants, domestic and wild animals and birds. The land, by being fallow, bore witness to Yahweh's ownership. The direct link between Yahweh and land was to be left intact; the land's rest was not disturbed by human intervention of tilling.

The second requirement was the jubilee tradition in Leviticus, which was concerned with the just division of land within Israel. It ensured that land allocated to certain clans could be reclaimed after a certain period. This involved the redistribution of land every fifty years, so that not only food was redistributed, but also the means of food production, the land. If the freedom of the nation was threatened by economic inequality, then those inequalities must be removed (Leviticus 25:10-14). The jubilee concept remains a yardstick by which one can measure programs of land reform today. The fundamental principle underlying this tradition is that the land belongs to God rather than to human beings (Leviticus 25:23-24).

When one speaks of the land as being a gift, then justice must be practiced in it. It is significant that Naim Ateek chose Moses' words as the title for his book on Palestinian justice—words pertaining to the land, "Justice, and only justice, you shall pursue, so that you may live and occupy the land that the Lord your God is giving you" (Deuteronomy 16:20). One cannot help but notice that Abraham was promised the land as a gift from God, but when he went to bury his wife Sarah, he paid its price to the Hittites (Genesis 23). In a later story from the time of the prophets, Naboth's vineyard is confiscated by deception and force of the governing authorities, Ahab and his wife Queen Jezebel (1 Kings 21). The prophet's instructions to curse in verses 17–19 show God's uncompromising concern for justice in the land. Canon Ateek writes, "Ahab knew that before God's law all people are equal, including the king. Yahweh's ethical law is in contrast to Baal's law. Yahweh, championed by the prophets, operated impartially; every person's rights and property and every life were under divine protection. Wherever injustice occurred, God intervened to defend the poor, the weak and the defenseless."[4]

People often give priority to the stories of the violent conquest of Moses' successors, Joshua and Caleb, and think that this is the preferred way of obtaining the land and even of monopolizing God's gift of the land. For Palestinian Christians they are disturbing and raise questions about the justice of God. Yet they cannot be ignored. From a historical-critical perspective, biblical scholarship has reminded us that we have no eyewitness accounts from the period of the conquest. The stories were only written down centuries later from the perspective of those already inhabiting and controlling the land. We are compelled, therefore, to try to penetrate the surface of the biblical words. When that is done, it seems that some later writers were intent on justifying their own status in the land on the basis of nationalistic perspectives. Other writers offered a critique and called for a reappraisal of nationalistic attitudes.

From a theological perspective the conquest stories can be read as the beginning of the downfall of biblical Israel—showing where the desire to conquer and possess stifles the life of faith in a good and gracious Lord. So while the book of Deuteronomy includes the descriptive instructions to kill all the Canaanites (Deuteronomy 7:2; 20:16–18), it counters with the reminder of the giftedness of land and the responsibility of inhabitants.

That's why I believe that the conquest stories must be read in view of the prophets. The biblical prophets were crying for justice in the land, and they refused to exempt the people of the covenant from the standards expected of the other nations (Amos 1–2). Inspired by God to apprehend and to proclaim the meaning of divinely guided events, the prophets brought a fresh understanding of justice to the land. I have found it helpful to chart out the parallels between the words of the original covenant and the words of the prophets as in the following diagram:

Development	Original Covenant	Prophetic Emphasis
Goal of the Covenant:	the land	righteousness + justice
Impediments:	"enemies"	sins
Conditions:	obedience	obedience

In the earlier period, the term *salvation* referred to military victory wrought by God's strong hand and outstretched arm (Psalm 136:12). In prophetic teaching, however, "salvation" means the spiritual blessing of true religion (Jeremiah 7:5-7, 13-15).

We can also notice that Amos, Isaiah, and Jonah present God as the God of justice for all, who desires goodness and mercy for all people living in every land. This universalistic point of view shows that God's justice starts from this land to every land. In postexilic Judah, Ezekiel expected Jews and aliens to live together with full rights guaranteed for all (Ezekiel 47:21-23). In Isaiah 61, the prophet appeals to Israel to reinstate the practices of sabbath and the jubilee year, which had fallen into disuse because of landowners' self-interest. The concept of land as a promised land ought to be the paradigm of justice, not of war and injustice. This is the prophetic message for every time and every place.

The Theology of Landlessness and Landedness

I have been strongly influenced by the work of the Old Testament scholar Walter Brueggemann who twenty-five years ago wrote his landmark study *The Land*. "The Bible itself is primarily concerned with the issue of being displaced and yearning for a place," he says in the opening chapter.[5] That rings true for Palestinian Christians. The Old Testament people of Israel are the perfect example of homeless people who were constantly on the way to landedness. Yet land always became a problem. "The very land that contained the sources of life drove kings to become agents of death. Society became the frantic effort of the landed to hold on to turf, no matter what the cost."[6] Thus the story is in constant movement from landlessness to landedness and back to landlessness.

Yet this is not just an Old Testament topic. The New Testament conveys the message that the birth of Jesus Christ is the ultimate fulfillment of the promise made to Abraham and of the hopes expressed by the prophets (Galatians 3:26-29; Matthew 8:10-12). The Christian church was preparing itself for the inbreaking of the ages, anticipating that a new era was about dawn. There are reminders in the New Testament, as Brueggemann notes, that socioeconomic-political concerns remain at the forefront: The Magnificat of Mary which speaks of the putting "down the mighty from their thrones" and the exalting of "those of low degree" (Luke 1:52); the symbolism of "kingdom"; the language of Jesus about saving and losing life (Luke 9:24); and the Sermon on the Mount blessings to the meek as the ones who will inherit the earth.[7]

Brueggemann notes the survey of W. D. Davies that the treatment of land in the New Testament is often ignored, spiritualized, or treated sacramentally and that it is displaced by the person of Jesus Christ.[8] Yet he deliberately goes beyond earlier views, claiming that "the proclamation of Jesus is about graspers losing and those who open the gifts as receiving."[9]

The key is in understanding the crucifixion and resurrection through the prism of land. According to Brueggemann, the person of Jesus himself "embodies precisely what Israel has learned about land: being without land makes it possible to trust the promise of it, while grasping land is the sure way to lose it."[10] His crucifixion embodies the movement from landed to landlessness. His resurrection embodies the movement from landlessness to landedness.

This theology of crucifixion/resurrection is the theology that helps the Palestinians at this very stage of history as they understand their relationship to the land. Interestingly, Brueggemann did not speak directly to the current Palestinian–Israeli conflict in his 1977 book. However, when a second edition was produced in 2002, Brueggemann added a lengthy preface and a final chapter in order to speak to current issues. "It is clear on any reading," he says, "that the modern state of Israel has effectively merged old traditions of land entitlement and the most vigorous military capacity thinkable for a modern state. The outcome of that merger of old traditional claim and contemporary military capacity becomes an intolerable commitment to violence that is justified by reason of state."[11]

The point of Brueggemann's study is that land is gift, not entitlement. Christians reading Paul's words in Romans 4 and Galatians 3–4 are given assurance that they are heirs of the promises to Abraham through faith in Christ. Yet heirs by grace, not by right. Thus a reminder that our place in the land is not as a replacement for the people of the old covenant, but as coheirs and coinhabitants who are called to live together in peace. Language of "claim," "entitlement," and "right" has no place in a theological discussion. The land is the Lord's and we together are its tenants.

What this means is that the issue of land is political, not theological. When someone occupies land "in God's name" and builds a settlement "in God's name," that places the guilt inappropriately upon God and not upon the occupiers or the settlers. Likewise, any idea of transferring one group of people for the benefit of another must be rejected.

The Land of Salvation

Biblical faith, however, should not be presented as a historical movement indifferent to place. It is not something that could have happened in one setting as well as another, because it is undeniably fixed to this very land of my birth. My colleague Monsigneur Rafik Khoury writes, "If there are favorable times when God intervenes with greater force, there are also places where God gives us rendezvous. There are places where God wants us to meet Him, thus corresponding to our human psychology on certain days, but we also try to have a rendezvous with Him in very specific place."[12] This goes for Jews and Muslims, as well as for Christians.

The Christian tradition has been very clear in locating the story in place and in time: in Bethlehem, in Nazareth, in Galilee, and in Jerusalem. As there is a history of salvation, there is a geography of salvation. This geography is in my land, the land of salvation. This is the reason that one often hears the land described as "the fifth Gospel."

The early disciples were called to be witnesses in Jerusalem, Judea, and Samaria. What happened once that witness moved "to the ends of the earth"? Two different perspectives are presented in early church writers concerning the Holy Land. Eusebius of Caesarea (260–340 C.E.) held to a spiritualizing of the land with little significance for the physical place. He said that the city of Jerusalem might be of great interest from a historical point of view, but theologically its significance in the present and future was nil. At the opening ceremonies of the Church of the Holy Sepulchre, built by Constantine's mother Helen, he deliberately focused attention away from the physical land to the powerful witness of the universal church.[13] In Alexandria at that time, Athanasius (296–373) reminded his fellow Christians in his annual Easter *Festal Letters* that their Lenten preparation was a "spiritual" journey to Jerusalem no less important and no less real than an actual physical journey.[14]

In contrast, Cyril (315–386 C.E.), who was bishop of Jerusalem just after the building of the great churches, understood that the theology of incarnation affects the theology of land. The place and land of salvation are themselves witnesses. "Many are the witnesses in the holy land," he said. "The place of the resurrection, the place of ascension, the angels who witnessed the events, the cloud with which he ascended, and the disciples that came from there."[15] Jerusalem has never lost its special significance in God's sight. Every stone is a witness. Pilgrims, therefore, were encouraged to come to Jerusalem in order that their faith might be revived.[16] It was Jerome, who traveled from Rome to live in Bethlehem while engaged in the Vulgate translation, who promoted pilgrimage with his letters to the West and through his assistance to travelers. To the Roman noblewoman Marcella he wrote in 386 C.E.:

> Time forbids me ... to recount the bishops, the martyrs, the divines who have come to Jerusalem from a feeling that their devotion and knowledge would be incomplete and their virtue without the finishing touch, unless they adored Christ in the very spot where the Gospel first flashed from the gibbet....
>
> Every man of note ... hastens hither.... They all assemble here and exhibit in this one city the most varied of virtues. Differing in speech, they are one in religion, and almost every nation has a choir of its own.
>
> As everyone praises most what is within his reach, let us pass now to the cottage-inn which sheltered Christ and Mary. With what words and what expressions can we set before you the cave of the Savior?
>
> Behold in this poor crevice of the earth the Creator of the heavens was born; here He was wrapped in swaddling clothes; here He was seen by the Shepherds; here He was pointed out by the star; here He was adored by the wise men. The spot is holier, I think, than that Tarpian rock [upon which the Temple of Jupiter was founded in Rome] which has shown itself displeasing to God by the frequency with which it has been struck by lightning.[17]

For Christians, the land of salvation remains the symbol that God worked in history and is still working in this land and every land. This land still witnesses to us and to every land, that after every form of suffering, there is resurrection.

The Land and the People

There can be no land without the people. The Old Testament presents a symbolic triangle that consists of God, people, and land, balanced to form their security and peace. However, we notice that the conquest under Joshua was so obsessed with the land that it sometimes forgot the other peoples. Did God really mean for the children of Israel to kill and massacre the other nations? Is it their nationalistic sentiment that led them to that or is it God's order? When I read the overarching message of the Bible of God's gracious acts for the whole world, it is difficult to conclude that this was God's will. When I read the book of Joshua I am struck by the prohibitions against acquiring individual profit. Likewise, the emphasis upon the distribution of tribes to various areas suggests not exclusive control of the land, but coexistence with the other nations—a picture implied in the book of Judges.

Canon Naim Ateek makes an important observation when he contrasts the first entry that took place during the time of Joshua and Caleb and the second entry from the Babylonian exile. The first saw the indigenous inhabitants as wicked people who should be slaughtered and displaced. The first was bloody treatment of the indigenous. In contrast, the people of the exile saw the indigenous people realistically as sharers of the land. The returning exiles were happy to accept a very small territory between Bethel and Hebron.[18] It is in the message of the postexilic biblical prophets that we see most clearly an attitude of equality among all peoples.

The Land and the Current Conflict

The present political conflict between Israelis and Palestinians is centered on the land. Since Leon Uris's novel *Exodus* and the popular motion picture based on it, a new mythology has been used to justify Israel's claim to the land. Modern Israelis become the true heirs to the promises to Abraham. Israelis are the people of a new exodus who will find peace and security only by occupying the land.

Where does that leave the Palestinians? If one side uses the biblical texts to justify expropriation of the land, then we must hear the religious arguments of the other side as well. Latin Patriarch Sabbah puts it well when he says, "If one of the three religions were to claim, in the name of religion, a political right to the land, then the two other parties would have the right to have the same claim, for the same reason. The three religions are the 'descendants,' physical and spiritual, of Abraham to whom God promised the land."[19] The two peoples, Palestinians and Israelis, have political rights to the same land; the three religions also have religious rights. The world has been faced with a dilemma for over half a century. This land belonged to one people for centuries, but now in the name of religion they are being dismissed and obliged to leave their land by various methods. The biblical land claims of Jewish and Christian extremists breed injustice for a whole nation. At the same time, it increases the sense of belonging for those expelled.

Since biblical times, this land always had a pluralistic population of peoples living along, side the Jewish people. Why should not this be the case today? The security of any nation lies not in confiscation of land or in exiling another nation, but only in building mutual relationships of trust. It is a possibility that exists only through justice. When peace negotiations refer to "land for peace," we assume that peace is secured only through a just solution concerning the land. The security of Israel is interdependent with the issues of justice in the land and freedom for Palestinians.

For Palestinian Christians, there is no other land for us than this land. It has molded our identity. The future of the Christian presence is in a just peace, not in occupation and war. We believe that we represent the continuity of the Old Testament and New Testament peoples' existence on the land. This is not merely an emotional attachment, but one that has geographical, historical, traditional, cultural, and social, as well as spiritual roots. We are tied to the land as the land belongs to us. We will exist and coexist as long as the land is also our land of milk and honey.

For Palestinian Christians, Jerusalem represents the navel of the world, symbolically located near the Holy Tomb in the Holy Sepulchre Church. Whenever we visit there, we make a point of touching this spot as a constant reminder of our place in the world. Our whole existence revolves around the belief in the crucifixion and the resurrection. It nurtures our faith that the hope of resurrection will overcome all suffering from injustice and oppression. The resurrection creates in us new life, revives love, promotes peace, and calls for reconciliation to live together in the land. It provides us the only lasting security, which frees us up to be witnesses, engaged fully in a pluralistic society.

Greek and Cypriot pilgrims have a custom that illustrates this special link to the land. Many visit Jerusalem at Easter with the intention of becoming godparents to a Palestinian child through the sacrament of Holy Baptism. They believe that they will be truly blessed when fulfilling such a vow. This is a reminder how place and people belong together. That's why many have come to refer to the Palestinian community as "living stones." The land is holy only with the continued existence of the living body of Christ.

Pope Paul VI wrote, "Those brothers and sisters who live where Christ lived and who still live around the Holy Places are the successors of the early church. They are the origin of all other Christian churches. They have done a great favor, and we owe them for this vast spiritual religion.... Were the presence of Christians in Jerusalem to cease, the shrines would be without the warmth of a living witness and the Christian Holy Places of Jerusalem and the Holy Land would become like museums."[20]

Christian emigration due to the political situation is a matter of real concern. The Christian presence is threatened. We as church leaders in Jerusalem are shouting and raising our voices as we feel that the church universal shares in this responsibility that the Christian witness endure in this land of resurrection. We consider our calling to be witnesses of the resurrection to be valid in Jerusalem until our Lord returns. Without the Palestinian Christian grass roots, there will be no Christian church in the Holy Land. The Holy Land will not be a holy land. We do not want a church of stones and a land without people, but a church of the living stones that sanctify the land by the ongoing preaching of the gospel and the administration of the holy sacraments. Our call is to be witnesses in the land.

5

Witness for Justice:
The Political Situation

"I dream that my people, the Palestinians, may really experience a just and secure peace." These words were part of my inaugural sermon as bishop on January 5, 1998. Integral to my call to be bishop is my role as witness for justice.

This was the witness of the Old Testament prophets. "What does the LORD require of you," asked Micah, "but to do justice, and to love kindness, and to walk humbly with your God?" (Micah 6:8).

Karl Barth notes, "God always takes his stand unconditionally and passionately on this side and this side alone: against the lofty and on behalf of the lowly; against those who already enjoy right and privilege; and on behalf of those who are denied it and deprived of it."[1]

Justice marks a follower of the way of God.[2] Amos spoke at a time of extreme inequities in Israelite society. Like Micah, he called for justice. "But let justice roll down like waters, and righteousness like an everflowing stream" (Amos 5:24).

Statement by Church Leaders on Justice

When the first Intifada erupted in December 1987, I was serving as parish pastor in Ramallah, a city faced with curfews and closures, a city where education came to a standstill and where every family grieved over tragic deaths and disabling wounds. The leaders of the thirteen Jerusalem churches wrote a common statement to show their solidarity with the oppressed and those suffering from injustice.

The recent painful events in our land which have resulted in so many victims, both killed and wounded, are a clear indication of the grievous suffering of our people on the West Bank and in the Gaza Strip. They are also a visible expression of our people's aspirations to achieve their legal rights and the realization of their hopes.

We, the heads of the Christian Communities in Jerusalem, would like to express in all honesty and clarity that we take our stand with truth and justice against all forms of injustice and oppression. We stand with the suffering and the oppressed, we stand with the refugees and the deported, with the distressed and the victims of injustice, we stand with those who mourn and are bereaved, with the hungry and the poor. In accordance with the Word of God through the prophet Isaiah, chapter 1, verse 17: "Learn to do good; seek justice, correct oppression; defend the fatherless, plead for the widow." We call upon the faithful to pray and to labor for justice and peace for all the people of our area.[3]

Peace Based on Justice

What does the Middle East need more than anything else in the twenty-first century? What is the most important thing that Israelis and Palestinians can wish for? The answer in one word—justice.

Many people would answer in a different way. What we need most is peace. "Pray for the peace of Jerusalem," we so often cry with the psalmist (Psalm 122:6). Yes, we all desire peace. But the biblical concept of peace is something much more than an end to conflict. It is more than getting along together and showing respect. Peace is a wholeness that is made possible by justice. Justice is the prerequisite for an enduring peace.

It has been estimated that in the twentieth century no fewer than fifty different peace proposals were offered to settle the Israeli–Palestinian conflict. They all failed. There has been no easy peace. The reason? They all failed to begin with the principle of justice.

Recently, Palestinians and Israelis have gone through a decade of intense peace negotiations. The result has been unparalleled levels of violence and ill will. In the popular media, these talks were characterized as "land for peace." The assumption was that Israelis would give up land while in return the Palestinians would guarantee peace. The problem is that the land that Israel was supposedly offering was not really theirs to offer—either from a theological or from a political point of view. Justice was short-circuited, and the peace talks were doomed to failure.

The assumption was similar to that addressed in Amos's day. Israel saw itself as a privileged people. Yet the prophets challenged that view:

> Are you not like the Ethiopians to me?
>   O people of Israel? says the LORD.
> Did I not bring up Israel from the land of Egypt,
> and the Philistines from Caphtor and the Arameans from Kir?
>   (Amos 9:7)

There are no privileged people. All must be on an equal footing.

All People Equal in the Eyes of God

The principle of justice begins with the assumptions that both parties in negotiations will treat each other equally, that there will be mutual respect, that each side will view the other as a gift from God. For Palestinians and Israelis, this equity is based on a number of factors.

First, both sides can affirm a belief that the same God created Jews, Muslims, and Christians, that all are endowed with the image of God, and that love for God is transferred into love for neighbor as oneself.

Second, this same creator God has provided the land with all its resources as a gift for the benefit of all these people. It is not to be squandered, nor is it to be used as a source of domination by one group over the other.

Third, both peoples have a long and rich heritage with roots in the land. To argue over who was in the land first or who had the longest claim or whose claim is more legitimate by differing theological standards is to deny the importance of the first principle. It is counterproductive.

Fourth, both peoples have the right of self-determination because of who they are, not because of events occurring in Europe or any other part of the world, not because any third party has granted them. It is a basic human right.

Fifth, Palestinian and Israeli census figures put the two groups roughly on an equal footing. With nearly five million Jews and five million Arabs, the two sides have equal needs for a reasonable livelihood.

A Solution Based on Justice

On the basis of this principle of equity, a solution can be negotiated based on international legitimacy, the Geneva Convention regulations concerning human rights, and UN resolutions. I have consistently supported the following:

1. **End to Occupation.** United Nations Resolutions 242 and 338 should be implemented, bringing about full Israeli withdrawal from Arab lands occupied in 1967. By signing the Oslo Accords in 1993, the Palestinians already relinquished to Israel land designated in the 1949 armistice—a very generous 78 percent of historical Palestine. There should be complete Israeli military withdrawal from the West Bank and Gaza. All security needs should be achieved my mutual consent.

2. **A Two-State Solution.** This solution goes back to the original United Nations partition plan in 1947, but it has, nevertheless, been denied to the Palestinians for over half a century. From the Palestinian point of view, full recognition of Israel has been assumed with the signing of the Oslo Accords iin 1993 and affirmed by the full assembly of the Palestinian National Authority in 1998. From the Israeli point of view, opinion polls have demonstrated that the majority of Israelis now accept the reality of a Palestinian state. I support two states living side by side, peacefully, equitably, justly, and being reconciled. A viable Palestinian state means that they have sovereignty and control of water and mineral resources in their territories.

3. **International Legitimacy.** The world community must recognize both Palestinian and Israeli states and support their coexistence in the land. Basically, UN Security Council Resolutions 242 and 338, and General Assembly Resolution 194, have done this. The matter must only be implemented. Because of the large discrepancy in per capita income, wealthier nations should be encouraged to invest and support the Palestinian economy. Special consideration should be made to restore the infrastructure destroyed in the current conflict.

4. **An End to Jewish Settlements.** All settlements in the West Bank and Gaza should be discontinued. Israel should be encouraged to resettle

these residents within Israeli borders. Any Jewish settlers who might remain by mutual consent should be dealt with under Palestinian law with both full rights and responsibilities in the same way that Palestinians in Nazareth and other Israeli locations are expected to follow Israeli law.

5. **A Just Settlement for Refugees.** Consistent with United Nations statements in 1948 and 1949 and with Resolution 242 made by the United Nations Security Council on November 22, 1967, there must be "a just settlement of the refugee problem." The 1947–49 combat created refugees numbering 750,000, many of whom continue to live with their descendants in refugee camps. Additional refugees were created by the 1967 war, some of them second-time refugees. One study estimates that the property losses incurred by the 1948 refugees total $169 billion in terms of the value of 1948 dollars.[4] Because homes were immediately bulldozed, and new occupants have taken over the land, a careful settlement must be reached. What does that settlement entail? I would suggest that the issue be divided into two important components. First, the world community and Israel must recognize that an injustice was created in 1948 for Palestinian refugees. Second, a just and reasonable settlement must allow for the right of return.

6. **A Shared Jerusalem.** The city of Jerusalem must be shared equally by both Israelis and Palestinians as two peoples and three religions—Judaism, Islam, and Christianity. East Jerusalem can be a capital for the Palestinian State and West Jerusalem for Israel. Such an arrangement would mean that Jerusalem is an open city. It is the view of the church that there must be access to the Holy Places in Jerusalem. Palestinians from the West Bank and Gaza should be given full and free access to Jerusalem for worship, for health care, for educational purposes, and for social purposes.

The Oslo Accords (1993) failed because they did not remain faithful to principles of justice. Palestinians were led to believe one thing, and Israelis another. For example, Palestinians expected a gradual withdrawal from the whole of the West Bank and Gaza, while Israel planned for partial withdrawals and continued settlement expansion uninterrupted during the whole peace process. This illustrates that the basic principle was one of political compromise rather than one of justice. Yet the most critical flaw was that the two sides were not treated as equals. Israel continued to be the party of domination, while subjection was assumed for the Palestinians. The result was less a movement toward peace than a respite from conflict. It was destined to be neither fully acceptable to either party nor enduring. It was not a peace based on justice.

The final downfall of the Oslo Accords occurred at Camp David during the summer of 2000, when the issues were hurried to the negotiating table without proper preparation. President Clinton pushed the issue of Jerusalem in a way that confused religion and politics—in a way similar to that of Old Testament king Jeroboam, whom Amos criticized for making Bethel into the king's sanctuary. Clinton focused the issue of Jerusalem—on the Dome of the Rock and the Wailing Wall—in such a way as to forget everything else about Jerusalem. When religion is used in this way, it often leads to a legitimization of power and a self-justification for continued injustice.

When the prophets spoke, it was always for justice in society and never for the politicization of religion. In a similar way, the church leaders of Jerusalem produced a joint statement in November 1994, "Significance of Jerusalem for Christians," that called for a shared Jerusalem.[5] It was a prophetic statement. How do we know? It was criticized by politicians on all sides, Israelis and Palestinians alike. The political solution seeks power and control. The prophet seeks justice for all.

The Issue of Jerusalem

Because of the complicated nature of the issue of Jerusalem, I am including in full a speech I delivered on the subject to the United States Senate—a meeting that was arranged by the Holy Land Ecumenical Foundation.

Both Father Majdi Siriani, representing Latin Patriarch Michel Sabbah, and I were invited to address senators at a special forum as part of the Jerusalem Committee at the Dirksen Senate Office Building on October 4, 1999. In the audience were representatives of the Arab-American and Jewish communities, as well as a significant number of reporters.

The title of my speech was "The Significance of Jerusalem to the Christian Churches in Jerusalem."

> Good afternoon. I am honored to be given the opportunity to share some thoughts with you on the significance of the holy city of Jerusalem for the Christian churches at this critical moment in history.

Jerusalem is significant for the church because it is the place of the life, death, and resurrection of Jesus Christ, the place where the Christian church had its origin. It is for the church throughout the world no mere relic of a bygone age, but a community that functions with vitality in the present day. It is the center of the church's life, the place to which it returns again and again to reaffirm its heritage and find strength for its renewal. It is for Christians throughout the world a place of pilgrimage, study, and meditation. It is in the shadow of the Holy Places that the church finds inspiration for its witness and service to the world.

As a Palestinian Christian who was born and raised in the Christian Quarter of the Old City, my family's home was a mere two minutes from the Church of the Holy Sepulchre and five minutes from the al-Aqsa Mosque of the Muslims and the Wailing Wall of the Jews. I have always felt that those Christians who live within Jerusalem had a special responsibility to carry the living torch of faith that is handed to us by the apostles and the early church.

Just as Jerusalem is dear to us Christians, however, I recognize that it is also dear to Jews and to Muslims. For this reason, it holds the possibility for the creation of both conflict and harmony, estrangement but also reconciliation. We Palestinian Christians have lived in Jerusalem since the time of the early church. We are composed of four families of churches, namely: Eastern Orthodox, Oriental Orthodox, Catholic, and the Evangelicals. At one time Christians comprised 15 percent of the population. Due to the unstable political situation, the Israeli closure of Jerusalem, confiscation of Palestinian residency permits, the building of settlements, and the absence of economic and cultural opportunities, however, the Christian population of Jerusalem has been drastically reduced. Out of a population of twenty-seven thousand in 1967, there are now only approximately eight thousand Christians in the city. If this trend continues, our churches will become museums. The very city that witnessed the birth of Christianity will have become a place devoid of a viable Christian presence.

As we approach the celebration of the two thousandth anniversary of the birth of Christ, a great many apocalyptic and millennial sects are taking a special interest in Jerusalem. These sects understand Jerusalem to be the place where a series of events will take place prior to the second coming of Jesus. Some of these groups, coming primarily from the USA, believe that it will be necessary to tear down the al-Aqsa Mosque of the Muslims in order to rebuild the third temple, thus hastening the second coming of Jesus Christ. These groups cause tensions and harm the good Christian–Muslim and good Christian–Jewish relations that the local Palestinian churches have established throughout the centuries. These groups abuse and misuse the Bible for their own interests. Jerusalem cannot afford such tensions. The Jerusalem we know is the Jerusalem of dialogue, the place of mutual acceptance and reconciliation. I fear that if Jesus comes again and sits on top the Mount of Olives, he will weep again with the words: "Jerusalem, if only you recognized the things that make for peace!" (Luke 19:42).

Jerusalem is a city to be shared by Jews, Muslims, and Christians alike. This is the position of the Christian Heads of Churches in Jerusalem. In November 1994 we issued a statement which took into account Israel's exclusive claim to Jerusalem as its unified, eternal capital, and the Palestinians' claim to East Jerusalem (presently "occupied territory" according to United Nations resolutions) as the capital of the future Palestinian state. I can summarize briefly that statement as follows:

First, Jerusalem is a place of equal, just coexistence for Israelis and Palestinians where their political aspirations may be implemented and where they will have their national, civil, human, and religious rights fully practiced.

Second, Jerusalem must be the place where Judaism, Christianity, and Islam must equally coexist and live their faith. Jerusalem must be a secure haven for all three monotheistic faiths. They must not only have free access to their Holy Places, but must enjoy the blessings of justice, equality, dialogue, plurality, and reconciliation in Jerusalem.

Third, the local Christian church is the local expression of the worldwide Christianity. For this reason, the local Christian communities, as the local Jewish and Muslim communities, should enjoy all those rights that enable them to continue their active presence in freedom and fulfill their responsibilities toward both their own local members and the Christian pilgrims from all over the world. Palestinian Christians, like all other citizens, religious or not, should enjoy the same fundamental rights, whether they be social, cultural, political, educational, and national. Among these rights are:

- the human rights of freedom of worship and of conscience, both as individuals and as religious communities;
- civil and historical rights which allow them to carry out their religious, educational, medical activities, and other acts of charity;
- their rights to have their own institutions for the study of Bible and traditions, centers for encounter with believers of other faiths, monasteries, churches, cemeteries, and so forth, and the right to have their own specialized personnel to run their institutions.

Fourth, the local Christians demand a special statute for Jerusalem. They believe that all the above presupposes a special legal and political statute for Jerusalem which reflects and emphasizes its significance. Experience shows that local authorities, for political reasons or the claims of security, are sometimes required to violate the right of access to Holy Places or the rights of other nations or communities. Therefore, it is necessary to accord Jerusalem a special statute which will allow Jerusalem not to be victimized by laws imposed as a result of hostilities or wars, but to be an open city which transcends local, regional, or world political troubles. This statute, established in common by local political and religious authorities of the three monotheistic religions, should also be guaranteed by the international community.

Fifth, it is also important that the local Christian churches be represented as observers during negotiations on the future status of Jerusalem in order to guarantee that these principles are adhered to. They have been accepted by the churches in Jerusalem and supported by the World Council of Churches, the Vatican, the Lutheran World Federation, the Anglican Communion, and many other Christian communities.

Finally, I would like to make an urgent request. It is that you vigorously oppose efforts that would force a move of the

U.S. Embassy from Tel Aviv to Jerusalem. I ask you to oppose any measure that would seek to change the status of Jerusalem prior to the conclusion of a negotiated agreement between Israelis and the Palestinians. As the facilitator of the peace process, the United States should avoid any action that would predetermine the outcome of the final status negotiations.

It is now the time of truth for Jerusalem. It is time that the United States use its influence to guarantee that the city of Jerusalem, the "City of Peace," be not exclusivistic but pluralistic in nature. It is my dream that Jerusalem will become a shared city for equal rights and responsibilities corresponding to the aspirations of the two nations, the Israeli and the Palestinian, and the three monotheistic faiths, namely, Judaism, Christianity, and Islam. There will be no peace in the Middle East without a just peace for Jerusalem. Jerusalem is the symbol and promise of God's reconciliation to all humankind. It can become a living paradigm of coexistence and reconciliation between two nations and three faiths. I ask you to help us to realize this dream for a shared Jerusalem. As a Palestinian Christian bishop, I urge you to work and pray for the just peace of Jerusalem.

May God bless you.

6

Witness for Nonviolence
and Moderation

My approach to life has always been one of nonviolence. From a theological perspective, I have always believed in nonviolence. From the very first chapters of the Bible, when God condemned Cain for killing Abel, it is made clear that human beings are not to live in violence. It is so integral to the teaching of Jesus that theoretical discussions on the Bible must always point to the way of nonviolence.

On a practical level, I have also always believed in nonviolence. Even as a child, I never sought to solve problems with my fists. Rather, I have always sought solutions by talking, by negotiations, even when those negotiations are long and drawn out. Sometimes this is the more difficult way. Nevertheless, conflict should always be settled by talking.

Many say that talking is the weapon of the weak. It accomplishes nothing. Besides, didn't Jesus take a whip and drive the money changers out of the temple?

Yes, I do not deny that episode, but this is one incident among many in his life. The overarching message that spans the years from his birth to his death, from his preaching in Galilee to his death in Jerusalem, is one of nonviolence. The Sermon on the Mount sets forth his message in no uncertain terms: blessed are the peacemakers; love your enemies; turn the other cheek. Jesus fought against the political and religious situation of his day with principles and doctrines, not with physical power. This led him to the cross.

Many years ago in confirmation class in Ramallah, a young boy raised his hand and asked, "If Jesus is truly God, why didn't he get down from the cross and slaughter them all right then and there?"

"Yes," I answered, "he would have shown himself to be God. Yet, this is not the way of the Christ, a way of witness and service through suffering."

In a similar way, I was once accompanying the archbishop of Sweden, K. G. Hammar, and his delegation for a visit to Yad Vashem, the Holocaust Memorial. In front of us was a group of Israeli schoolchildren. One raised his hand and asked the guide, "I don't understand. Why didn't the IDF [the Israeli Defense Forces] shell the Germans to stop them from killing the Jews in Germany?"

Of course, there is a humorous vein to this story because of the confusion in chronology. But the lesson to be learned from this child is the idea that arms are the answer. To this young Israeli, weapons are now the solution for every situation. What will happen in the future? Can children who grow up with these ideas consider other solutions? What will happen ten, twenty years from now when peace is established, and there are two neighboring states of Israel and Palestine?

A violent society is self-destructive. Dr. Martin Luther King Jr. reminds us that the ultimate weakness of violence is that it is a descending spiral begetting the very thing it seeks to destroy. Instead of diminishing evil, it multiplies it. He said, "Returning hate for hate multiplies hate, adding deeper darkness to a night already devoid of stars. Darkness cannot drive out darkness; only light can do that. Hate cannot drive out hate; only love can do that. Hate multiplies hate, violence multiplies violence, and toughness multiplies toughness in a descending spiral of destruction."[1] When one works for freedom through the way of arms and power, what will come when that freedom is achieved? Will those participants in the struggle themselves be freed from violence? Or will they be so captivated by violence that they can never live together in true peace?

Violence and the Occupation

The principle of nonviolence is important now in the struggle to end occupation. The church views the occupation itself as violence against the Palestinian people, violence that takes many forms.

There is daily physical violence inflicted by Israeli soldiers "to keep order," as they say: the shellings, the shootings, the beatings.

There is emotional violence when soldiers daily humiliate grown men and women at checkpoints, forcing them to their knees, abusing them with words of hatred, and stripping away their human dignity.

There is violence in the denial of basic human rights like water, homes, and health care.

There is the violence of terror. When Israeli helicopters shelled the town of Beit Jala, the children were left with psychological problems. "Mommy, will they shell us again tonight? If I go to sleep, will I wake up again?" Every time these children hear the sound of a helicopter, they tremble because of the possibility that shelling may resume.

There is economic violence as closures prevent people from going to work and force them to live on an average of two dollars a day in poverty. UNRWA estimates 60 percent current unemployment and two-thirds of the population living on less than two dollars a day.[2] They do not have the income of their land. They are forbidden to harvest their crops, and their lifelong investments of property are destroyed.

And there is violence of the word. Every day, the media portray the Palestinian people as a violent people who only want to cause trouble. They are described as parents who send their children purposely into the line of fire. To the world, Palestinians are seen as terrorists. They are not portrayed as real human beings. Those who misuse words also must be held accountable for this violence.

The church speaks out strongly against this violence of power that humiliates the weak—the violence of military occupation. The world needs to speak out. Occupation is a sin against God and against humanity because it deprives the "other" their dignity and their right. It is destruction first to the occupier, then to the occupied. God gives land as a gift to promote life, not to support domination of the strong against the weak. The World Council of Churches has declared 2001–10 "the decade of nonviolence." It speaks directly to our situation as Palestinians. They have also initiated the program "End the Occupation."

In the struggle against apartheid in South Africa, participants faced the same manipulation of the word *violence* that occurs both in the media and in Israeli and Western government statements concerning the Israeli–Palestinian conflict. It was the South African church that called attention to this issue in the *Kairos Document*.

> The problem for the church here is the way the word "violence" is being used in the propaganda of the State. The State and the media have chosen to call violence what some people do in the townships as they struggle for their liberation, i.e., throwing stones, burning cars and buildings, and sometimes

killing collaborators. But this *excludes* the structural, institu-
tional, and unrepentant violence of the State and especially the
oppressive and naked violence of the police and army. These
things are not counted as violence. And even when they are
acknowledged to be "excessive," they are called "misconduct"
or even "atrocities" but never "violence." Thus, the phrase "violence in the townships" comes to mean what the young people
are doing and not what the police are doing or what apartheid
in general is doing to people. If one calls for nonviolence in
such circumstances one appears to be criticizing the resistance
of the people while justifying or at least overlooking the violence of the police and the State.

Is it legitimate, especially in our circumstances, to use the
same word "violence" in a blanket condemnation to cover the
ruthless and repressive activities of the State and the desperate
attempts of the people to defend themselves? Do such abstrac-
tions and generalizations not confuse the issue?[3]

There is a popular Arabic saying, "When you push the cat into the
corner, it scratches." This is what occupation does to the Palestinian
people. Yes, it is true, there is violence among the Palestinians. Some
people turn to violence because they are desperate, and they see no
other way out. Some people turn to violence because this is what they
have learned from the occupiers. They see that force has been successful in the oppression of this people; perhaps, they think, force is the
only way to throw it off. Former Israeli security chief Ami Ayalon spoke
out in October 2000, shortly after the beginning of the al-Aqsa Intifada.
"What can you expect if we point a rifle at the head of the Palestinian
and if we destroy the infrastructure for economic life? We cannot expect
them to act peacefully. As Israelis, we cannot live without the Palestinians. We have a relationship of symbiosis."[4] The current situation
has escalated so that the level of violence on both sides has become intolerable. I would claim that any violence on either side is intolerable.
But, violence has come to rule us.

The church cannot condone this. The church must provide a witness of nonviolence for the Palestinian people. The church must stand
up and point to the way of nonviolence as the only viable solution.

In his interview with *Le Monde,* Ayalon asks why the number of
Palestinian "terrorists" is on the increase, according to Israeli army sta-

tistics, at the very time when the army is wielding its power against Palestinians as never before. When some say that the solution is for Palestinians to lay down their arms, this is to misunderstand the situation. The violence of occupation is the root of the problem. Those who oppose violence must speak for an end to all forms of occupation.

There is a fine line here that we must walk. Condemning the violence of Palestinians cannot be interpreted as passive acceptance of the occupation. Condemning the violence of Palestinians must always be linked to a harsh condemnation of the violence of occupation. And this is my approach. All violence must come to an end, on both sides. All forms of violence, including the occupation itself. To follow the way of nonviolence can never mean abandoning the way of justice. Both go together.

The principle of nonviolence is important now in the struggle to end occupation. It is an equally important principle as we look to the future. How will we Palestinians live together in a future civil society? How will the Israelis live with their internal differences? How will these two neighboring states coexist in this small piece of land?

Our prospect, therefore, must be twofold. First, how do we end occupation? Second, how do we build a civil society among Palestinians? We must always be thinking further than postoccupation. Discussions now must focus on a constitution for a democratic society, on a state of law, on structures and institutions that will guarantee the freedom and human dignity for everyone.

Education for Peace

One of my questions is, After we are freed from occupation, will the world still be interested? Will the world still be offering the support and encouragement that it offers us now during this struggle? Take, for example, South Africa and Namibia. Ten years ago, the attention of the whole world was focused on southern Africa and the quest to end apartheid. Now what? The struggle there is to build a nation, but they are seemingly left alone.

The church's goal, then, is not only to end the injustice but also to build a just society. In this effort, there is nothing more important than peace education. Some people think this is something we can deal with later, after we have a Palestinian state. Yet, the educational struggle is as important now as the political struggle.

One of the issues is the matter of security. A rabbi who is my dialogue partner needed to travel for a meeting in a Palestinian area of Jerusalem. "Will you guarantee my safety?" he asked.

"Sure, of course," I told him. "You will be perfectly safe. You can trust me."

All of his life, this rabbi has been so bombarded with images of violent Palestinians that he is genuinely afraid to enter their neighborhoods. We must condemn the media's violence in perpetuating such one-sided images that provoke only fear. So, my rabbi friend is genuinely concerned about security. Although he is committed to nonviolence, he may still think it is better to remain separated, living only among Jews. In our dialogue, however, he has come to trust me as an individual. He knows that he has nothing to fear. And now he is gaining confidence to travel with me among Palestinians to meet Palestinians and eventually to come to trust them, too. This is peace education.

In the same way, how many Palestinians have known only "violent" Israelis? At one time, there was much more interaction. Yet look what the occupation has done! Through closures, the number of Palestinians working for and alongside Israelis has been diminished. The typical Israeli has become for the Palestinians the one they confront at checkpoints – the soldier with a gun – or the undercover agents who operate in the Palestinian areas. Because of this power dynamic, Palestinians have come to hate Israelis. Palestinians are not anti-Semitic. They are anti-occupation. They are anti-domination. They are anti-oppression. Israelis represent these conditions to the Palestinians.

Even in the Old City of Jerusalem, many of the Israelis encountered by Palestinians are carrying weapons for protection. It is sad that they feel insecure to walk the streets of the city of peace. Yet, because of their insecurity, their weapons reinforce for the Palestinian the image of forced occupation.

Recently, my wife and I were preparing to walk to my mother's house in the Old City from Jaffa Gate, where we customarily park our car. An eleven-year-old Jewish girl stood there speaking in Hebrew: "I am afraid. I want to go through the Old City to the Jewish Quarter, but I am afraid that an Arab will stab me."

Since Suad knows Hebrew, she addressed this girl in Hebrew and offered to accompany her. "No one will hurt you," assured Suad.

"But my teacher said that Arabs will harm me," the girl protested, obviously afraid.

Nevertheless, she was willing to trust Suad, and she accompanied us down David Street through the suq until we reached the Jewish Quarter—having gone a bit out of our way. When we were about to separate from her, Suad asked, "Did you feel safe? Were you threatened by anyone along the way?"

"No, I was quite safe. Thank you," she answered.

"Good," Suad responded. "You do understand that we are not Jewish, even though I speak Hebrew. We are Palestinians. Shalom."

The girl stood there with her mouth hanging open. She had been educated to fear Palestinians and had thus avoided them. This day, she was given a lesson in peaceful coexistence. Such lessons are needed if there is to be hope for the future of our two peoples.

On another occasion, two young Israeli lovers were walking by Redeemer Church. Arm in arm they walked, young and in love. It was a wonderful picture of youth, love, and hope for a long future together. Yet over the young man's shoulder was slung his machine gun. This is abnormal for any society. Lovers and a gun. It is not how we were meant to be.

For fifty years, we in this land have had an armed struggle. What has it achieved? Nothing. Only hatred has grown stronger, not security.

Nonviolence—A Shared Path

In 1988, when Yasser Arafat declared that he accepted a two-state solution—that Israel and Palestine must recognize the right of existence for each other—and again, when he signed the Oslo Principles of Understanding, he expressed an important conviction. He said, "We are more powerful when we are negotiating." The opposite, too, must be said. We are weakest when we use force and violence.

The late Israeli Prime Minister Yitzhak Rabin came to the same understanding. During the first Intifada, his policy and his public statements were well known. "We will break the limbs of those who resist," he said in addressing the situation. Yet there was a *metanoia,* a dramatic turning around, a recognition that such strategy only increases violence and does not offer a lasting solution. For Rabin, negotiation also became the answer.

Rabin made an even stronger witness. His message of peace through negotiations became so strong that it threatened those who sought solutions through a gun. His assassination by a fellow Israeli is an unforgettable tragedy. Yet the gun did not silence Rabin. His message became even stronger in his death. Rabin was a true "martyr for peace" because he challenged the views of many Israelis.

It is no accident, then, that whenever violence seems to show its ugly, frightful head, low-level government figures move into action. They realize that even the violent rhetoric of leaders will move them no closer to solutions. It is only through negotiations. The word is more powerful than a missile.

The way of nonviolence has proven itself successful in many parts of the world: in India with Gandhi, in the U.S. civil rights movement with Dr. Martin Luther King Jr., in South Africa and Latin America. Many have compared the Palestinian struggle with the successful campaign against apartheid in South Africa. They have encouraged us to continue walking the way of nonviolence.

Yet, some have noted a difference. In the Palestinian struggle, the Christian element is but a minority. "Can this road of nonviolence be successful in a Muslim community?" they ask.

I would challenge this suspicion. I am a minority as a Christian. However, I am not so sure that I am in the minority as a proponent of nonviolence. I don't see myself as being on the fringes of Palestinian life. Rather, I am part and parcel of a Palestinian society that is composed of many different views.

It is true that Christian communities in various parts of the world have played prominent roles in bringing about change through nonviolence. Yet, Christians certainly do not have a corner on the nonviolent movement. Who was Gandhi, after all? Again, such suspicions may reflect the image encouraged in the media that Muslims are a violent people, that they are terrorists, and that they willingly send their children to violent deaths.

In traditional Arab society, how are problems solved? Not with a sword, but with negotiation. This is the concept called *al-Sulha,* which means "reconciliation." Often it involves a very long process with lots of discussion, for which, if I am not mistaken, Arab culture has much more patience than the Western demand for instantaneous results. An essential element in the process is the selection of an honest broker who works for the best interests of all. All parties understand that he will speak truthfully. Each group will speak to him as the mediator. When justice is granted through this group negotiation, it is final and lasting within the community—much more effective than the judicial system. In the end, he declares the amount of compensation—referred to as "ransom." Then, the perpetrator is required to bring the "ransom" himself and present it to the family of the victim.

They ask him, "How much?" He gives a figure.

They respond with a higher amount.

"No, by the prophets," his side traditionally pleads.

"Okay, we forgive you," the victim's family announces.

The eldest member of each side then symbolizes reconciliation by kissing one another. Afterward, they sit and drink coffee. The *Sulha* does not mean only emotional reconciliation, but a sincere effort to give full rights.

Were an individual not to accept the decision but to resort to violence, he or she would be shunned by the community. For some reason, many seem to forget this side of Islam. Yes, there are many Muslims who join me in the path of nonviolence. As just a single example, one can turn to the daily nonviolent demonstrations led by Hanan Ashrawi and other Palestinians when the Israelis seized the Palestinian Authority's offices at the Orient House in East Jerusalem in the summer of 2001.

At the same time, it is necessary to recognize many Jews who walk this road with us. My many friends in Rabbis for Human Rights have been very supportive over the years, often at great personal risk. Likewise, there are movements such as Peace Now—former army generals who have altered their views—and Women in Black. At the Jewish athletic Maccabee Games in Jerusalem in the summer of 2001, eight Israeli women protested simply by holding up signs that questioned the role of occupation and the violent response by the Israeli army. The women put themselves at risk in a hostile crowd and were escorted under force from the stadium. In Beit Jala, Israelis helped to organize a program with international human rights activists to stay in Palestinian homes under fire from Israeli tanks. In Beit Shuafat and other locations in Jerusalem, Rabbis for Human Rights have protested unceasingly against home demolitions aimed at Palestinian families. It is not unusual for Israelis and Palestinians to come together for nonviolent demonstrations against the occupation.

A few years ago, I was invited to participate in a panel discussion by the Olof Palme Peace Center, which included members of the Swedish parliament, on "No to Violence and Yes to International Legitimacy." When I finished my thirty-minute presentation, the moderator announced that there was no time for questions. I could see, however, that there was a person anxious to talk. I told the moderator, "Please, we should allow at least this one man."

He stood up and began to speak. "I am thirty-one years old and, like all Israelis, served in the IDF. I manned the checkpoints. I roughed up and detained many Palestinians. I entered many of their homes with the force of my gun. Only when I came to Sweden did I begin to understand the Palestinian point of view. If more Palestinians would speak the way of this bishop, I think more would be persuaded to end the occupation. What I did was wrong. I will never serve in the army or stand by force again. I commit myself to working for human rights."

This statement by a former Israeli soldier gives me much hope. We need an awakening of the Israeli conscience. This must be the goal of nonviolent resistance. The way of the gun is so noisy that it drowns out voices of nonviolence. Violence only turns the other side against us and closes their ears so that they do not hear. The way of nonviolence shows them that we are human beings like them. It appeals to their conscience and their standard for what is right and what is wrong. It awakens them and then awakens others like a chain reaction. It demonstrates that this is not a struggle between Israelis and Palestinians, but a struggle between the way of power and domination and the way of nonviolence.

The lines of the struggle are thus drawn differently, so that there are Palestinians and some Israelis fighting for the same goal, just as Palestinians and Israelis are both living in fear. Note that I continue to speak of this as a "struggle" and say that we are "fighting" for an end of occupation. Nonviolence does not mean that we passively surrender to the evil of occupation. To the contrary, we work all the harder. Nonviolence and the fight for justice always go hand in hand. The church believes that occupation is self-destructive, a sin against God and against humanity. So, we will continue to resist, and we will continue to speak out against the injustice of occupation. We have the same goal as the entire Palestinian people: to end the occupation.

After Occupation

Where we go after the end of occupation may be more difficult. As I said before, we must have a two-pronged goal: the end of occupation and the building of a just Palestinian society. Some say that we can only focus on the first and that once occupation has ended, then we will worry about the second.

Yet, is that possible? If we follow the way of force now, will we be able to change later? Will the end of occupation achieved by force lead to peaceful coexistence and sharing the land? Or will it lead to further conflict with our neighbors? Will it lead to further problems within our own Palestinian society? This is why we need peace education now. This is why we must teach the way of nonviolence as the means to end occupation, so that we will continue to follow this road in building our nation.

Here is a point where, I think, the world totally misunderstands the current Palestinian leadership. During the current Intifada, the rhetoric in Israel is that Arafat is a terrorist, that Arafat is a man of violence, that Arafat is not a partner for peace. Prime Minister Sharon, seeking to discredit Arafat, declared that he is "irrevelant." Similar ideas are echoed through the rest of the world, only somewhat toned down: "Only if Arafat stops the violence can there be peace."

There are several problems here. Foremost is that we see the Israeli occupation as the root of violence. The occupation is powerful, it rules by domination, it is by nature violent itself. Yet, for those who believe in rule by the gun, any opposition, any resistance, any struggle, is interpreted as violent. So the Palestinians are labeled as violent, and the Israelis are seen as acting in self-defense. Their actions are described to the world as retaliatory and preventative, whereas in reality they are purely and simply violent. It is a strange way of thinking. I don't understand how domination of one people by another is excused as necessary force while the resistance to that domination is always labeled as violence.

As I write in 2002, Israel has moved to the extreme. The Sharon government presents a platform of domination and rule by force and reprisals to stamp out all resistance. Negotiation is in name only. It really aims at nothing but submission and compliance. Even peaceful demonstrations concerning the occupation within Israel proper have become a threat, and the government responds as a police state where human rights have been pushed into the corner.

What does the Israeli government want from the Palestinian Authority? It would appear that this extremist government seeks only a mirror image of itself. The ideal for them would be a police state in which dissent is not allowed and in which the Palestinian police must crack down with an iron fist and in which opposition must be imprisoned and silenced. In this view, ironically, we are expected to be a people of the weapon, only it is the weapon in the hands of a few who control the rest. Such a model is nothing but a police state.

According to this view, peace will come not with the end to occupation, but with the transfer of occupation to an authoritarian Palestinian figurehead who does the bidding of the Israelis. The Palestinian police would be no different than the Israeli soldiers. They have only changed uniforms. It will be a rule not through justice and democratic ideas, but through domination by force.

Some might call this peace. There may indeed be a decrease in violence on the surface, so that the world can smile and award peace prizes to the victors. But it would not be a peace based on justice, and it would not be an enduring peace. The cry for justice would continue beneath the surface. It would only be a matter of time until another uprising began. Perhaps it would be put down by force. But it would be followed by another, and then another. Rule by force simply will not endure. Justice and truth can never be silenced; eventually they will win.

As I see it, the position of the Palestinian Authority has been designed to be inclusive of all political factions. Some seek negotiation. Some seek confrontation with the weapon. Some seek democracy. Some seek rule by a few. There are multiple views in Palestinian society. If the goal is to create a democratic state, can it wait until after occupation is ended? Or is it a process that must begin now? If the latter is the case, then it must be a rule not only of the majority, but in which the minority views must be respected as well. Human rights for all must be protected. This is the difficulty with the democratic method—and remember, we are new to democracy in the Middle East. It takes time and patience. We must learn from our mistakes.

I truly believe that the Palestinian people as a whole want a voice of moderation and will reject the voice of extremism. I believe that the way of negotiations will be chosen over the way of the weapon. Unfortunately, the root problem has not been dealt with. The occupation has not been removed. The Oslo peace process reshaped and remolded it, but still the occupation has remained. If those are right who say that violence begets violence, then what has the violence of occupation begotten for us? The voice of the weapon has become stronger on the Palestinian side in response to continued occupation. In return, the voice of the weapon has become louder still on the Israeli side. And so on. It is a never-ending spiral.

This is why the voice of nonviolence must insist on justice. It cannot compromise on the question of the occupation. Nonviolence must witness to the end of occupation.

Witness to Hope

I could easily be discouraged. When I write this, it seems like the way of the weapon is winning the day. Yet it also seems that whenever the situation escalates, people on all sides seek more fervently for alternatives. Now, more than ever, I must promote the way of nonviolence. Now, more than ever, the way of nonviolence has a real future.

Many examples encourage me and nourish me in this effort. I will later tell the story of Suheila Andrawes, who hijacked an airplane at gunpoint. Her lesson is that weapons in the end accomplish nothing. "I will continue to fight," she says, "but now with the word." The same insight now guides the Israeli soldier whom I met in Sweden. "What I did was wrong," he said. "I commit myself to working for human rights."

I think, too, of the witness of those who have died. My cousin George was a victim of violence, as I shall describe later. Yet his funeral proclaimed not vengeance, but the need for Muslims, Christians, and Jews to work together for peace.

One of the most moving stories coming out of the struggle to end occupation took place during the current Intifada, when a thirty-three year old Palestinian pharmacist from Shuafat named Mazen Joulani was shot in the head and killed while sitting at a café in East Jerusalem. According to AP wire service reports, it was suspected that the drive-by shooting was carried out by an Israeli settler. The family, dedicated to the peace process, wanted to do something to make a difference. This was not the first time tragedy had struck the family. In 1998, when a cousin from Aida refugee camp in Bethlehem was killed by bullets from IDF troops, the family donated three organs to Israelis. Now, even though violence had escalated between Israelis and Palestinians, they again announced that they would offer his organs for transplant. As Muslims, that was a difficult decision. Yet five organs, including his heart, were donated to save the lives of others, no matter who they were. "Islam does not forbid donating organs to save another's life," said the aged father, Lufti Joulani. "So, I donated organs to save the lives of others, no matter if they were Jews, Christians or Muslims."[5] It turned out that four went to Israelis and one to a Palestinian. Today five people have better lives because of this gift.

A young Israeli father of two, Yigal Cohen, would have died had he not received a heart transplant from Joulani. "This is a noble act that really, really touched us. We were very surprised yesterday to find out the identity of the donor," Cohen's father David told Israel Radio. "It is really touching, especially in these days when relations are so tense, this noble family comes and teaches us that it is possible to do things in a different way. The very fact of the act simply taught me that there are other kinds of people on the other side and maybe there will be others like this, and through people like this we will find the path to peace and to a normal relationship."[6]

This Muslim family followed the path of nonviolence. The witness they gave cannot but help to awaken the conscience of the Israeli people and all people throughout the world.

Witness for Moderation

Christianity, Judaism, and Islam are all religions of peace. The terms *shalom* and *salaam* used in daily greetings in Hebrew and Arabic are reminders for those of us of a Christian background that the primary focus is on peaceful relationships among individuals who reveal God's own image within them.

At the same time, it is not difficult to cite examples where individuals, movements, and entire nations have misused religion to achieve their political goals. How can a group of people steer planeloads of innocent people into a skyscraper, killing another three thousand victims, all in the name of religion? How can someone such as Osama bin Laden issue a call for Muslims to join together in a holy war against the West? Such extremism uses religion as a justification for domination, prolonged injustice, and violence. As a church, we must speak out against such extremism in religion and promote moderation.

Christians in self-critical fashion can cite the Crusades as an example of religion's misuse to justify political goals of Europe in the Middle Ages. The crusader movement was a perverted pilgrimage to Jerusalem, and they perverted the cross. They were colonialists who had no intention of bringing religion to this country. They are no different than Caleb and Joshua. God never told the Israelites to go and kill the women and children and chickens. They used religion to achieve political goals.

The crusaders are still in the mind of the Muslims. Sometimes local people talk about Christians as the new crusaders. The European crusaders actually harmed the indigenous Christians. We have to be ashamed of that period. The Christians here, of course, sided with the local people, both Muslim and Jew, against the crusaders. They comprehended that this had nothing to do with religion. It was a political war in the name of religion. Perhaps as a reminder of their own self-interest, the crusaders founded many new pilgrimage sites like Rachel's tomb at locations convenient to their travel, not based on historical considerations. They simply perverted religion in every way to accomplish their own self-interests. Thus, it was only appropriate for President George W. Bush to backtrack quickly after speaking of a "crusade" when calling for a war on terrorism. His move acknowledged that both ideas, holy war and crusade, are extremist.

From Secular to Religious

The current Palestinian–Israeli conflict is marked by religious extremism on all sides. Yet it was not always that way. The first Zionists seeking a homeland for the Jews were pragmatists who were not motivated by religious concerns. They simply wanted a place where Jews could live in peace away from the threat of anti-Semitism. They originally considered locations other than Palestine. Even after the Holocaust, the movement to Palestine was controlled by secular Jews, and religious Jews refused to support the move to statehood. From the beginning, resistance to Jewish immigration and statehood was based on the growing movement of pan-Arabism and the national aspirations of Palestinians, not from religious motivation.[7]

Today, we have religious fanatics on all sides. There are Jewish settlers who claim "God gave me this land" and then defend it with a gun. There is Rabbi Yusef of the Shas party who describes Palestinians as scorpions and who currently has introduced seventeen anti-Christian resolutions in the Knesset. There is Baruch Goldstein, a member of the Kiryat Arba settlement, who on February 25, 1994, gunned down twenty-nine Palestinian Muslims as they were praying in the Ibrihimi (Abraham's) Mosque in Hebron. There is the Muslim suicide bomber who believes that God will take him to paradise for killing Israelis. There is an extremist Muslim sheik who speaks hatred against Israel and calls for a jihad to conquer the land. There are extremist Christian apocalypticists who see the establishment of the state of Israel as a fulfillment of ancient prophecy and part of an end-time countdown leading to a nuclear conflagration at Armageddon.[8] There are Christian fundamentalists who march around Jerusalem like Joshua, praying for the destruction of the Dome of the Rock so that a third Jewish temple can be built in anticipation of Christ's return.

There are Jewish fanatics calling for an all-Jewish state in all of Palestine and transfer for Palestinians. There are Muslim fanatics who are calling for an Islamic state, not just in Palestine but in the whole Middle East. There are Christian fanatics who say, "We need a common Christian front and combat all other religions."

Tolerance and Intolerance

We are all living in a world torn between tolerance and intolerance. The tension between the two is a very serious one. As we view our world, we notice the prevalence of intolerance, both by followers of other religions and by adherents of our own religion. This intolerance can be seen in a very conspicuous way. When the Islamic Taliban movement insisted on destroying the great Buddhist monuments in Afghanistan, the world reacted. When they heard the outcry from the Western world, Muslims were asking, "Why did the world not react the same way when the al-Aqsa Mosque in Jerusalem was set on fire some years ago or when another mosque was torn down in India?"

Adherents of various religions sometimes use their holy writings to justify intolerance or injustice in our violent world. We need not look further than within Christianity, where fundamentalists justify Israeli occupation of the Palestinian territories as being part of God's fulfillment of the Old Testament's prophecies.

Religion can become a tool, misused by extremists who adopt intolerant positions or biased attitudes. These groups can easily become a threat to world justice and peace, and create turmoil. These extremist groups succeed where poverty and injustice prevail. Likewise, they grow when violence against them rules the day. Their strategy is to be the advocates of God—though in the end, it is a perverted God created in their own image. In the Middle East, which is a fertile ground for fundamentalism, these groups find a lot of muddy water where they can swim.[9]

People tend to judge other religions by the historical and existential standards of their own religions. In this way, tension is created among the religions. Pride in one's own religion leads a person to be intolerant of the other. Nowadays, Islam is the fastest-growing religion in the world. Yet many descriptions by outsiders are based on observations and judgments concerning Islam as it is practiced by extremist groups, not as Islam is normally understood. Following the September 11 attacks, evangelist Franklin Graham, the son of the famed and well-respected Billy Graham, declared that Islam is "an evil and wicked religion." The same tendency holds true for Judaism, which suffered for centuries in Europe. It was judged by the behavior of some of its adherents, not by its teachings and doctrines. This created prejudice and fear from followers of other religions and brought unwanted extremism. Today, as a Christian in the Holy Land, I perceive that the growing perception of Christianity is based on the actions and words of Christian fundamentalists and not on the teachings of the long-established churches. There is much misunderstanding among religions today.

Religious Fanaticism

We are challenged and obstructed by religious fanaticism and extremism. The religious fanatic often claims to be motivated by a desire to see his or her religion return to its "original" or "pure" state—as that person sees it. Yet, the fanatic generally pursues this self-assigned goal by rigid application of "original" values to contemporary practices and observances without recognizing that the "originals" were part and parcel of a differing age and culture.

What is a fanatic? In my view, a person who has "indoctrinized" his or her own personal interests. Finding something from one's own political ideas or in one's own personality justifies this thinking to make it a religious ideology. In dispensationalist theology, is it Christ's desire to bring about Armageddon or is this the preference of the fanatic? Or, what kind of God does the Christian fanatic have who claims, "God ordered the state of Israel to do this to the Palestinians"? If that person's child were a Palestinian, could the same thing be said? I doubt it. These are self-interests to justify their own identity. At the time of the millennium, an apocalyptic group from Denver settled in Jerusalem with the goal of bringing down the Dome of the Rock to make room for the third temple, in order to hasten the second coming of Jesus and in order that two-thirds of the Jews might be massacred at

Armageddon. As a Palestinian Christian, I would not like that even for a moment. This is a degrading use of religion that I cannot accept. It's genocide. It's racism. It's fanaticism. We condemn religious fanaticism. We condemn racism. We condemn discrimination. We condemn apartheid. Yet, this country is very fertile for fanaticism.

Cardinal Francis Arinze said in a lecture in Jerusalem that extremism is often characterized by an intransigent attitude toward coreligionists and others who hold different views or who practice another concept of society.[10] This frequently leads to violence. Some extremists go even further, denying the right to religious freedom to those whose religious convictions differ from their own.

How can we carry out our mission in such a world? How can we be witnesses when religious intolerance is growing? Christian mission is prohibited by law in some Islamic countries. In Israel, there have been laws against evangelizing Jews since 1977, and new ones are currently being proposed. Yet, we are called to be witnesses.

Response to Religious Fanaticism

What shall I say as a Palestinian Christian who is a moderate? There is a growing fear that there will be an Islamic state and a Jewish state, while the Christians will be left in between or outside. It seems that Anglican Bishop Riah Abu El-Assal was right in his book *Caught in Between*.[11] What kind of states will Israel and Palestine be in the future? We cannot ignore it. We cannot say, "We don't want to speak about it." And we cannot hide under the pretext that we are one Palestinian nation. As a Palestinian Christian bishop, I must address the issue and resist any such avoidance.

At the same time, we must be careful not to overplay the issue of fanaticism. If we are fanatical in our response, it will only serve to increase the problem. Fanaticism breeds fanaticism. It is important that we remember, too, that the Palestinian Christian community in general is not fanatical. Most people are moderate in their thinking, but you do find among us the fanatic element. I am a moderate. And as a good Christian and a good Palestinian, I can fight for my case better by being inclusive than by being exclusive.

For this reason, we as a church have to call upon Christians, Muslims, and Jews to speak for moderation. As Christian moderates, we can distinguish easily the Christian extremists because we know our own religion. Yet, when we are more ignorant about the tenets of both Judaism and Islam, we often find ourselves falling for stereotypes that take the extremists as the norm. As a first step, we need to grow in our understanding of both Judaism and Islam. A survey by the Lilly Endowment prior to the September 11 events found that only a third of American colleges and universities offered courses in Islam.[12] Congregational members throughout America and Europe likely have even fewer opportunities for such education. The church must take the lead in providing educational opportunities. Then, we need to enter into dialogue with moderate Muslims and Jews. Finally, we need to stand together to condemn fanaticism of every kind.

It is impossible to read the whole Bible and come away with the view of a God who breathes wrath and condemnation for all but a select group of people. Did God really tell Caleb and Joshua to come and kill all these people? Is God a God of vengeance? I don't think so. God is always a God of love. Individual self-interest creates a God of vengeance, who will do what we ask. Caleb and Joshua wanted to promote a tribal God, a God of exclusiveness, not one of inclusiveness. All the promises that were given to Abraham and others about the promised land—not to be read in a symbolical way—were given to the people to show that God is a God who keeps promises, unlike the idols. It was not given so they would believe that God blesses occupation. The Canaanites, the Amorites, the Jebusites—God created all of them. God is not against people but against idols. The intent was to have the Israelites live side by side with the other nations of the land under the living God. They were people elected to a duty and a responsibility, not to privilege. Their calling was to proclaim the living God to the other nations, so that this small nation could be a beacon of love. But it was perverted to exclusiveness. Then, as now, we turn religion into ideology. This is the tendency of all, and we must learn from the mistakes.

It is not unusual that when the Palestinian community in Hebron is under attack, Muslim leaders telephone me asking for help. They would not approach me if they were truly fanatics. And if I were a fanatic, they would not ask me. It is our call to help whoever is in need, regardless of nationality, or sex, or religion. That's what it means to be a witness. When someone calls me at night and asks for help as though we were good friends—although that is not necessary—I respond. Fanaticism can never be answered by fanaticism. Fanaticism can be answered only by openness and inclusiveness. And for me, this is a theological issue, not just an issue because of goodwill and nationalism. It is a deeply theological issue.

Jesus never answered fanaticism with fanaticism. He never went to the Pharisees and said, "Oh, you are fanatics, I am not interested in you." For the woman who was taken in adultery, he wrote on the ground; he did not attack them directly (John 7:53–8:11). In Matthew 23, see how he replies with "woe" to those who are exclusivistic. When the Syrophoenician woman said, "See the crumbs," he said, "No ma'am, you don't need to eat crumbs, eat bread" (Mark 7:24-30). Similarly, he offers living water to the Samaritan woman in John 4. In the Old Testament, the book of Jonah demonstrates that narrow-mindedness and fanaticism will never take you further than your own thinking.

Principles for Christian Witness

I strongly believe that dialogue eases the tensions in the world. At the same time, I also believe that Christian mission is to witness to the reign of God. But, this should never be done in a coercive way or by force.

We are to present our faith in our Lord Jesus Christ as being as simple as it is. Christianity has certain barriers to dialogue. Some are rooted in our own convictions, such as exclusive truth claims. Others consist of heavy historical baggage that we still have to leave behind and make amends for, such as anti-Semitism, xenophobia, colonialism, sectarianism, racism, sexism, and attitudes of cultural superiority.

As a Palestinian Christian, I subscribe to the following basic principles in mission, developed in a World Council of Churches Multifaith Consultation on Religious Education.

- The doctrine of creation is expressed in the equal value and human rights of everyone. God created every person in his image worthy of full human rights.
- The doctrine of incarnation is to be presented as the willingness of God to engage himself fully in humanity and restore its dignity.
- The compassion of Christ is revealed in dialogue that acknowledges and addresses the suffering of others.

- The prophetic tradition challenges injustices.
- We work together with all people of goodwill for reconciliation and love.[13]

As Christians, we have a great challenge to be witnesses in a violent world. Are we ready to see God in the other? Are we ready to accept the otherness of the other? This is the witness of moderation.

Part III
Applications

7

Witness in the Face of Terrorism

September 11, 2001, marks one of the worst tragedies in American history. Four teams of terrorists hijacked domestic flights to bring about unparalleled destruction. Two flights crashed into New York's World Trade Center, turning this symbol of Western economic power into a pile of rubble. Another flight crashed into a wing of the Pentagon, symbol of U.S. military might. The fourth plane crashed in an unpopulated area as passengers subdued the hijackers. Over three thousand persons died, their lives cut short unnecessarily. Hundreds of thousands of relatives and friends suffered the loss of loved ones. The entire American nation suffered a loss of innocence and was left feeling vulnerable, violated, and uncertain about the future. The American people did not suffer alone. The whole world suffered with them.

I know. I suffered along with the American people.

I happened to be in the United States at the time of the attacks. A week earlier I had stood on a stage at Wartburg College in Waverly, Iowa, to receive an honorary doctorate. Addressing my audience with my vision for a just peace in the Middle East, I felt hopeful and encouraged about the future. When I first learned of the WTC attacks, I was stunned. I was in California for a clergy conference. It was obvious that everyone there was shaken by these tragic events. Americans had experienced before what it is to be a victim. On the previous Memorial Day, the film *Pearl Harbor* was released to present to a new generation of Americans the event that brought them into World War II. Only months earlier, Timothy McVeigh had been put to death for his role in the Oklahoma City bombing. News of investigations about the attack on the USS *Cole* was still fresh in the minds of many. Yet, there had been no parallel to the scope and extent of the September 11 attack. So it was only natural that all those around me in California were hurting.

I know. I was hurting with them.

At first, it was not clear who was to blame. One of the first reports suggested that Palestinians were responsible for the attack—a speculation that was soon retracted. Others reminded the American public that the terrorist Timothy McVeigh was a Caucasian Baptist. Still, as events unfolded over the next several days, it became clear that the perpetrators all were Arabs, and they all were Muslims. The honor of decent Arabs and Muslims suffered as a result of the selfish acts of a few.

I know. I suffered with them.

A number of commentators remarked that now Americans understand what it means for Israelis to be victims of terror. So many Jewish families have suffered greatly from suicide bomb attacks on innocent victims going about their daily lives. They know that a human life suddenly cut short can never be replaced. They know the empty spot left in their lives as they try to move on. They know sorrow. They know pain.

I, too, know what it means to be a victim of terror.

Victim of a Suicide Bus Bombing

My cousin died in a suicide bomb attack on a Jerusalem bus. George Younan was a thirty-eight-year-old carpenter who grew up in the Old City near the Latin Patriarchate. He was deaf and dumb, a gentle person who never caused anyone problems. He was employed by an Israeli who liked George very much. To get to work in the suburbs of Jerusalem, George typically took the 6:30 A.M. Egged bus on Jaffa Road in the Israeli section of West Jerusalem. This was one of the busier bus routes. George was always very careful. Sometimes when he sensed something wasn't right, he would come back home.

One Sunday, however, he did not return home. His fate was to be the victim of a suicide bomb attack. It was March 6, 1996, the second straight week of deadly attacks aimed at disrupting the peace process.

The implementation of the Oslo Accords had progressed relatively well through the fall of 1995. One by one, various Palestinian communities had been granted autonomy, and Israeli troops had withdrawn as a first step in the peace process. Yasser Arafat and Yitzhak Rabin appeared on the White House lawn in September 1995 to sign the Oslo II

Accords for further extension of the transfer of land, for which they received the Nobel Peace Prize. Then, extremists on both sides went into action to scuttle these accomplishments. In November, an Israeli, Yigal Amir, assassinated Prime Minister Rabin. The following February and March, Hamas carried out a series of bus bombings in Jerusalem and elsewhere in Israel. These eventually assured the failure of Shimon Peres's campaign for election as prime minister and led to the deterioration of the peace process. It was the second straight Sunday morning bombing of a number 2 bus on Jaffa Road when my cousin was killed.

We mourn all the victims whenever such an attack occurs, whoever that person may be. Many, of course, have been Jews, as is well publicized in the media. Less well known is the fact that a number of Romanian migrant workers had been killed in a bus bomb attack the previous Sunday, February 28. On March 6, among the dead were three Christians: a Syrian Orthodox woman from Bethlehem, an Ethiopian Christian woman from Jerusalem, and George Younan, a Roman Catholic.

I first became aware of the bombing around seven o'clock in the morning as I was dressing for church in Ramallah. When I saw the report on the television, I sat down for a moment. "Those poor people," I said out loud, calling my wife. I had no idea who the victims were. When you see such a report, you never think that it might be someone you know—a relative, a friend, a colleague. Still, the sight of such a tragedy brings forth emotions of deep sadness, because these are human beings. "Those poor people," I kept repeating, unable to express myself in any other way.

After a little while, I went to church in Ramallah, where there was the typical discussion about the news. Everyone without exception felt sorrow for what had taken place. Yet it was still early, and the reports were still fragmentary. As is the case in an area where tragedies like this are frequent, life goes on. We had our church service—I think it was Women's Unity Week, and the women of the congregation led the service, but I remember nothing else.

As is our custom, our family drove to Jerusalem to have Sunday dinner with my mother. Then, a phone call came from my uncle. "Munib, George is missing. He did not come home." We began to realize that this tragedy had reached out to touch our lives.

"*Ami* [my uncle], did you call the police?" I asked.

"I called," he responded.

"*Ami*, did you call the hospitals?"

"I called."

I put on my jacket and ran across the Old City through nearly deserted streets to his house near the Latin Patriarchate.

"I have already sent your brother Michael and your cousin Samira to Tel Aviv," he announced at the door.

"You think he may have been killed?" I asked, not really thinking of my words. At times like this, there is a thin line of hope. It seemed that he might have been killed, but maybe—just maybe—not. We waited.

Finally, Michael telephoned from Abu Kbir Hospital in Tel Aviv. "They received us here at the hospital with every courtesy," was how he began. We knew the reason for this, and we knew what he would say next. "They showed us first his ID card. Then they took us to the morgue to see the body."

We were all in shock. You never expect this sort of thing to happen to your own family members. Nevertheless, I had the sense first of all to call the entire family together to discuss how it was necessary for us to respond, because we all knew the press would soon be upon us. "Be careful what you say to the reporters," I counseled them. "First, it would be best if we had only one spokesperson for the family. Second, it would be best if everyone were on his or her guard not to say anything that might cast blame on the Muslims. The press will do their best to drive a wedge between us and to make this a religious issue. A Muslim did not kill our cousin. The political situation killed him."

Within minutes, the reporters were knocking on our door. "How does it feel to have a Muslim kill your family member? What do you plan to do to respond to the Muslims? Does it bother you to have this done by a Muslim?"

I was proud of my uncle. In the midst of his grief, seventy-five years of age, he was able to compose himself before the cameras. "The blood of my son, now mixed with the blood of Jewish children and Muslim children together, is shouting for peace and justice in this country. May God forgive those who did this and killed my son."

My uncle's words were shown on all the television stations. It was a powerful Christian witness.

Still, the reporters continued to hound us, looking for a way to find us in a weak moment or to trip us up. Finally, I pleaded with them, "Please, go! Let us grieve the loss of our cousin."

According to custom, we had scheduled the funeral for the next morning. It was difficult because with the closures we did not know if all the family members would be able to arrive from Beit Sahour and other places. We had the coffin ready at the family house, and it was something of a shock when they brought the body in a black plastic bag. Then we saw the body, and all stopped what we were doing. His hands were up as if to protect his face. His mouth was wide open. The expression on his face looked as if, for the first time in his life, his ears had been opened to hear the sound of this terrible blast. The police reported that he was in the process of boarding the bus at the very moment the explosion occurred. We pondered the irony of the situation until the priests came to take the body.

All the while, the press continued to hound us with their questions. I said, "Please, don't you understand, we want to grieve. We have experienced loss. We want to mourn our cousin's death."

They asked the same questions over and over again. "Don't you have anger toward the Muslims?"

The funeral itself took place at the San Salvador Basilica. The church was completely full with Palestinians—both Christian and Muslim—and also Israelis, including some of my Jewish dialogue partners and some of George's fellow workers. Death has a way of breaking down these barriers of religion and race.

Yet, there was also politics. Israeli Mayor Ehud Olmert of Jerusalem arrived and went directly to be seated with the patriarch and priests in the raised area around the altar. The cameras focused on him, and it seemed as if it was all for show. Then, some youths came running to me saying, "Why do you allow him to sit there like that? Does this show proper respect for Faisal Husseini?" Husseini, the late symbolic Palestinian figure of East Jerusalem, had seated himself below with the rest of the congregation.

"I don't care," I responded. "At this moment, I am only mourning my cousin." Then, they took Husseini and escorted him up to altar to sit across from Olmert with the Latin patriarch and priests seated in the middle.

The burial took place in the Catholic cemetery on Mount Zion. We were all prepared for a bombardment of further questions and requests for television interviews. Suddenly, the press disappeared in a flash. What happened? A report had come in that another suicide bomb attack had taken place that Monday afternoon in Tel Aviv. They were chasing another story.

A little later at the house, one of Michael's Israeli coworkers from Tel Aviv appeared to be disturbed. "What is wrong?" we asked.

"I am sitting and afraid. You see my daughter takes that same bus every day in Tel Aviv."

Immediately, we all forgot about our grief for George, and for a moment our concern was for a neighbor in need. "Please, take our telephone and call," we offered. That was before everyone carried their own cell phones. Then, the friend found relief. His daughter was safe at home.

Three days later was the traditional memorial service in the Catholic church. I was invited to preach.

"We are now mourning. We are sad. We are filled with pain and suffering," I told the congregation. "But we must tell the world that we have no anger in our hearts. There is no revenge. We do not know those who killed. In reality, it was the political situation that killed my cousin. Lord, forgive them, for they do not know what they are doing. Let George Younan be a martyr for peace. May we speak a message of forgiveness! May we all be committed to work for a just peace for all the peoples of this land!"

Later, they discovered that the bomber in the Jerusalem bus attack was a young man from Jenin. The press called to report this fact and to get my reaction.

"Please, I do not need even to know his name," I told them. "I forgive everyone. The situation is the problem."

In these circumstances, we find our role as living witnesses. Some see this role as one of weakness, but people can visibly see forgiveness taking place. There is really power in weakness. This was seen clearly as our Lord forgave from the cross.

We forgive as family, not just as individuals or as a church. Pain is still in our hearts. Yet that pain can never be quenched in vengeance. Pain will be quenched when peace comes, and we live together. Pain motivates me to work for justice, peace, and reconciliation even more fervently in a nonviolent way.

I have also been encouraged by the voices of Israelis who have been victims of terrorism. About a year and a half after George's death, in September 1997, a thirteen-year-old Israeli girl, Smadar Elhanan, was killed by another suicide bomber in Jerusalem. Her mother, Nurit Peled-Elhanan, has been a longtime advocate for peace and nonviolence. Clearly, such a senseless murder has tested Nurit's resolve. Yet instead of turning vengeful, she has sought healing through her continued efforts at reconciliation. During the time that she was grieving, the Palestinian Authority asked to send a representative to the funeral and to give her official condolences. She willingly agreed to receive the Assistant Deputy Minister of International Cooperation (planning minister) of the PA, Anis al-Qaq. The moment was captured by television cameras as he told her, "Your pain is our pain."

Then, the Israeli prime minister's office contacted her, saying that he would like to visit her. She refused. "Why do you receive this Palestinian minister, but do not receive Benjamin Netanyahu?" she was asked by a reporter.

She has related this incident on a number of occasions to Israeli women's groups during the current al-Aqsa Intifada. "When my little girl was killed," she stated, "a reporter asked me how I was willing to accept condolences from the other side. I replied without hesitation that I had refused it: When representatives of Netanyahu's government came to offer their condolences, I took my leave and would not sit with them. For me, the other side, the enemy, is not the Palestinian people. For me, the struggle is not between Palestinians and Israelis, nor between Jews and Arabs. The fight is between those who seek peace and those who seek war. My people are those who seek peace. My sisters are the bereaved mothers, Israeli and Palestinian, who live in Israel and in Gaza and in the refugee camps. My brothers are the fathers who try to defend their children from the cruel occupation, and are, as I was, unsuccessful in doing so. Although we were born into a different history and speak different tongues, there is more that unites us than that which divides us."[1]

When I hear her story, I am touched deeply. This is not about Palestinians and Israelis. It is about human beings who seek life. In this, Palestinians and Israelis are joined together against the current political situation, which seeks to rule by force and ultimately brings death, suffering, and destruction.

Every time I hear on the radio or on television that another bombing attack has taken place, my emotions are aroused from deep within me. It is as if I am reliving that moment when I heard about my own cousin's death. For this reason, I am reminded that these are all human beings. They all have families. Regardless of religion, ethnicity, or political affiliation, they all suffer and feel pain. I cannot help but feel concern for them. I feel physically sick in my stomach whenever I hear these reports.

When it comes to death, there is no Jew, no Muslim, no Christian. We console each other as human beings in suffering. We are all one.

Palestinians to Americans: "Your Pain Is Our Pain"

When Palestinians heard of the September 11th World Trade Center tragedy, they were moved deeply to express their sorrow. This is only natural. The number of Arab-Americans is significant. Many Palestinians have relatives living in the States. Just as important, Palestinians understand what it is to suffer.

Nevertheless, we must be alarmed at the repeated television images showing Palestinian children celebrating at the news of the bombings. Our alarm is twofold.

First, it is alarming that anyone could celebrate the misfortune of a fellow human being. This is not acceptable. While I am not trying to explain this behavior, I do believe it is important to stress that this was only a minority response—a small minority at that. By far, the greatest number of Palestinians truly mourned the American tragedy.

Second, our greater alarm must be expressed at the American media for presenting this image as if it were representative of the Palestinian people in general. The real tragedy is that the media continue to view Palestinians as terrorists and to prolong that view even when Palestinians are the victims of violence, whether it be by the Israeli army or by vigilante settler groups. This stereotype of Palestinians as terrorists is likely the reason American television was quick to report uncritically the rumor that Palestinians were behind the World Trade Center bombings. More representative of the Palestinian people are the images of Yasser Arafat donating blood for the victims, schoolchildren in the West Bank standing for a moment of silence, and young *hejab*-wearing Muslim girls holding a candlelight vigil outside the U.S. Consulate in Jerusalem.

This is why I have shared my own story, to emphasize that we truly understand the pain that Americans have experienced at the hands of terrorists. This is also why I immediately telephoned my secretary in Jerusalem, Mr. George Awad, to dictate a letter to the American people addressed through ELCA Bishop H. George Anderson. I thought that it was important that the letter originate in Jerusalem and that it be sent already on September 12 even though I was still in the States. Here is the letter.

Dear Bishop Anderson,

Salaam and grace to you from a troubled Jerusalem in the name of our Lord and Savior Jesus Christ.

On behalf of Bishop Munib Younan, I would like to express the ELCJ's deepest sorrow and strongest condemnation for the atrocious attack and savage act of terrorism on the World Trade Center in New York and the Pentagon, Washington, D.C., whereby thousands of innocent people lost their lives. In a telephone conversation this morning, Bishop Younan, who is currently traveling in the United States, expressed his deep personal shock and feeling of sympathy with the families of the victims. He affirmed his belief that we in the Church cannot give in to the forces of extremism, but have to give our support to the forces of moderation.

Bishop Younan, on behalf of all the members of our Church, would like to express to you as the spiritual leader of our sister Church, to the members of the Evangelical Lutheran Church in America, and the entire American people our solidarity and condolence. Your pain is our pain. We were shocked to watch this unprecedented act of violence and terrorism. We therefore share your sadness and sorrow for the loss of so many innocent lives.

We pray for you, and express our solidarity with all the families and relatives of the victims.

We take refuge in God's promise to unfailingly be with those are in need of His enduring presence.

Respectfully yours,
George Awad
ELCJ Church Secretary
On behalf of Bishop Munib Younan
Currently on travel in California, USA

I was not alone in expressing my condolences. Our pastor in Bethlehem, Mitri Raheb, circulated the following letter on behalf of his congregation and the staff of the International Center in Bethlehem.

With deep sorrow and profound grief we write this message to offer our heartfelt condolences to the mothers, fathers, children, friends and families of the thousands of innocent people who have been the victims of the terrorist attacks yesterday morning on the USA. We would like to reach out to all of our American friends to assure them that we stand by them at this difficult and tragic time. Constantly, for the past eleven months, we have received many messages from our friends from America expressing their solidarity and sharing with us our grief. Never in our worst nightmares did we imagine that we would be witnessing such a horrendous event and human tragedy inflicted on our American friends. We care for every life and we pray for all those who are mourning the loss of loved ones taken away by this indiscriminate act of organized terror. Our thoughts and prayers are with you all.

We are aware that the media has shown President Arafat's shocked reaction to this act and his strong condemnation of it. Unfortunately, the media has also shown scenes of a few Palestinians celebrating this tragedy. We want you to know that these few do not speak for or represent the entire Palestinian people. What the media failed to acknowledge was the majority of Palestinians who were shocked, saddened and mournful. We believe that this media campaign is biased and aims at dehumanizing the Palestinian people. Such a campaign follows the same logic of the terrorists, since it deliberately attempts to punish innocent people indiscriminately. In our grief, we are asking ourselves why did the people immediately associate us Palestinians with the perpetrators rather than the victims?

As Palestinians, we can very well understand the pain of our American friends. We know what it means when political leaders are targeted and are not safe in their own offices. We understand what it means when planes attack security headquarters. We know how it feels when the backbone of the economy is assaulted. We do not want to compare suffering, since every suffering is unique and this particular tragedy has such hideous dimensions. Yet, never before have Americans and Palestinians shared so much.

We express our solidarity with the American people. We invite people all over to:

hold vigil prayers for the victims and their families;
raise awareness and sensitivity to the brutality that the
    media perpetrates through the images projected;
monitor the way that certain nations and peoples are
    stereotyped (The Americans, The Palestinians, etc.),
    thus inciting hatred and legitimizing aggression;

develop alternative media that will set new ethical
   standards in reporting;

actively participate in the WCC's "Decade to Overcome
   Violence" so that future generations will have
   compassion, do justice and value life;

commit to prophet Micah's vision that "they shall sit every
   person under his vine and his fig tree and none shall
   make them afraid";

commit to this so that no American, Palestinian, Iraqi,
   Israeli, Japanese, or any other people will be afraid to be
   in his/her office, home, or airplane, no matter what
   nationality they hold.

May the peace of Christ be with us all.
Rev. Dr. Mitri Raheb, Pastor
Christmas Lutheran Church, Bethlehem.

Similar letters could be produced from various other Palestinians,
as well as Arabs and Muslims throughout the world, who grieved over
the American suffering. Reverend Sandra Olewine, Methodist liaison in
Jerusalem, reported visiting the American Consulate in Jerusalem,
where she was shown a stack of similar fax and e-mail messages twelve
inches high. In suffering, there are no divisions of nationality, or race,
or religion. In suffering, we are one.

8

Witnessing to a Terrorist

In response to the September 11 World Trade Center bombings, President Bush declared a war on terrorism. As evidence was gradually gathered, responsibility pointed in the direction of the al-Qaida network and specifically to Osama bin Laden. American and British military forces targeted terrorist bases in Afghanistan. The unofficial slogan soon emerged of the goal being "to get Osama."

In the process, various questions were raised, even by the American public. How does one distinguish between issues of justice and vengeance? Did justice require that bin Laden be punished by a violent death on the battlefield or be captured alive? If the latter, was it more proper that he be tried in an American military tribunal or in an international court of justice? More fundamental was the question whether bin Laden himself was beyond redemption. Was it still possible that he could be changed? Was it proper to pray for him? Was forgiveness possible? This issue is especially important for Christians because Jesus taught love of enemies and offered forgiveness to those who crucified him.

When one considers the case of Osama bin Laden, the issues are presented in the extreme. However, in most cases, the issues are more complex. What about the young disillusioned Saudi whose motives are less clear? What about the young American John Walker Lindh who sought adventure and made unfortunate choices? What about the young Palestinian whose father was killed by Israeli soldiers, whose home was destroyed, and who has despaired of any hope for the future?

The war on terrorism is sometimes blurred because terrorism itself is not easily defined. As it has often been said, one man's terrorist is another's freedom fighter. It depends on whose side one is on.

When one considers the Israeli-Palestinian conflict, the complexity of roles surfaces. Menachem Begin and Yitzhak Shamir were often considered terrorists because of their activities against both the British and the Palestinians prior to 1948. Later, both served as prime minister of Israel. In the view of many, Yasser Arafat was a terrorist because of his leadership of the Palestinian Liberation Organization during the 1960s and 1970s. Later, he was instrumental in the peace process and was awarded the Nobel Peace Prize (as was Menachem Begin), while being recognized as the legitimate leader of the Palestinian Authority. Ariel Sharon was stripped of his position in the Israeli government in the 1980s and formally charged with war crimes for his role in the Lebanese Sabra and Shatila refugee camp massacres. Later, he was the duly elected prime minister of Israel. In the Middle East, times and situations change. People change. Their roles may change.

The political context in the land of Palestine has led to bloodshed and violence. The Holy Land has been painted blood red by those involved in the struggle and by those caught in the way. In a sense, nothing has changed since those early days in the Acts of the Apostles when Jesus called his followers to be witnesses. The call itself sends us out into the world exposed and vulnerable. We are called to follow Jesus, even to die. Likewise, we are called to follow with a message of grace and forgiveness.

In this chapter, I share the story of a onetime terrorist who now witnesses her faith in Christ and advocates a message of nonviolence. I share my story as one called to witness to that message of Christ's forgiveness and reconciliation.

The Story of a Palestinian Terrorist

The story of Suheila Andrawes is a powerful story about repentance, forgiveness, and the gift of the sacrament. It is also an example of *martyria*—of witness to a person who is a suffering victim.

Suheila Andrawes's family originally came from Haifa and, because of the 1948 conflict, she grew up as a refugee in Lebanon. During the early 1970s she, like many young women of her day, turned to political activism with a nationalistic spirit and joined the Popular Front for the Liberation of Palestine (PFLP). As she reflects back on her youth, this was the equivalent of joining the Palestinian military at that time, and she was a young soldier.

In October 1977, she and three other PFLP members were given in-structions to hijack Lufthansa Flight 181 departing from Majorca, Palma. It was one of the most publicized hijackings of the decade. *Time* and *Newsweek* magazines gave the story seven and eight pages of cover-age, respectively. It was the cover story for *Time*. For *Newsweek*, the headline read "The New War on Terrorism."[1]

The purpose of the hijacking was to call attention to political pris-oners and to gain their release. As Suheila recalls the episode, her in-tent was not to cause harm or to kill passengers, but to use them as leverage to achieve a political goal. Nevertheless, lives of innocent per-sons were put at risk and, as often happened, the situation turned violent. The Lufthansa pilot and all three of her fellow hijackers were killed.

The ordeal lasted 110 hours. The scheduled short flight which took off at 1:00 P.M. on October 13 from Majorca to Frankfurt was diverted first to Rome, then to Cyprus, then Bahrain, then Dubai, and then Aden. By this time it was October 16, and nerves were frayed. In Aden, authorities had placed barricades across the runway, causing the pilot Jürgen Schumann to land the plane in the sand nearby. This led to a major outburst of anger from the leader of the hijackers. The pilot went to check the wheels to see if they would be able to attempt a take-off. When he returned, the leader accused him of causing the problems and after a brief argument responded by shooting him in the head.

The copilot then flew the plane to Mogadishu, where Somalian President Siad Barre agreed to let German authorities handle the situa-tion. In an eleven-minute raid, British and German commandos gained control of the plane, killing the other three hijackers. Suheila's body was riddled with seven bullets, mostly targeting her knees. She was carried from the plane on a stretcher and turned over to the Somalian authorities.

Suheila was taken to a hospital for treatment, tried in a Somali court, convicted, and sentenced to twenty years' imprisonment. She served two of those years in a Somali prison. However, because of the severity of her wounds, the Somali president ordered her release from prison and her transfer to Prague for medical care. There she remained for another one and a half years to undergo knee-replacement surgery and treatment for her injuries. At that point, she was freed and allowed to return home. Suheila reflects that there was never any discussion of her being returned to prison, or of her transfer to German authorities, or even of her traveling to a German hospital for treatment. Germany had apparently agreed that the government of Somalia was responsible for her. Because of the severity of her injuries, her behavior, and the time already served in prison, Suheila Andrawes was declared a free person.

At that point, life returned to normal for Suheila Andrawes. She returned to Lebanon, and in 1983 she married in the Greek Catholic Church and began family life with a child born around 1985. In 1991, the couple left Lebanon first for Syria and Cyprus and then for Norway, where they settled in the town of Grefsen. There, Pastor Svein Raddum became an important figure in their life, and the family became members of the Lutheran church. They learned the Norwegian language, and the two became incorporated into the community. Mr. and Mrs. Abu Matar and their daughter Laila were assumed to be a typical family. They were well liked and accepted by everyone. No one knew anything about their past.

Coincidentally, it turned out that the Lutheran Church of Hope in Ramallah had established a partnership relationship with the parish of Grefsen and participated in periodic exchanges. In 1993, my wife, Suad, participated in such an exchange and visited Grefsen. There she met Suheila and her family. Suad had grown up in Haifa, Suheila's family home, and the two became friends who continued their contact by correspondence. Occasionally she telephoned, and I, too, had gotten to know her by talking on the phone.

In October 1994, Suheila's life changed once again. At the request of the German government, Norwegian authorities detained her in prison for fourteen months while the courts worked through papers to extradite her to Germany for trial. Hers is a most unusual case. A Norwegian professor, Anders Pratholm, has written a book that challenges the legality of the whole proceedings. His primary argument, of course, revolves around the basic legal principle that a person should not be tried twice for the same crime and that the German government had made no attempts in the previous nineteen years to extradite her. He notes especially the timing of these events shortly after the signing of the Oslo Accords that emphasized the need to forget the past and to move on with the establishment of peace between Israel and the Palestinians. He also notes an inconsistency with the parallel case of the Israeli Mossad agent Sylvia Rafael, who assassinated the Palestinian Ahmad Boushiki at Lillehammer, mistaking him for a leader of the Palestinian resistance named Husan Salami. For this crime, Sylvia was convicted by Norwegian courts and sentenced to serve five years in a Norwegian prison. After one and a half years, she was freed, was married to her Norwegian lawyer, and was granted Norwegian citizenship. When Italy later wanted to extradite Sylvia Rafael because she carried an Italian passport, Norway refused. The past was forgotten. She was free to move on with her life.

Not so for Suheila Andrawes. Although courts in Oslo twice found that the extradition request was illegal, the Norwegian minister of justice intervened by naming a new judge to the case. In one week—the previous judge had studied the issue for six months—a ruling sent Suheila to Hamburg, Germany, in November 1995 for trial. Three charges were brought against her: first, that she had participated in the hijacking; second, that she had participated in killing the pilot; and third, that she had attempted to kill the commandos raiding the plane. In 1996, Suheila was found guilty and sentenced to twelve years in prison in Hamburg.

The Witness of the Gospel: Even to a Terrorist

Throughout the ordeal, Pastor Raddum continued to serve as Suheila's spiritual counselor. As early as her detainment in Norway awaiting the extradition decision, she requested through Pastor Raddum to see me as a Palestinian pastor. The foreign minister of Norway agreed. In 1996, I traveled to Norway and was taken by the Norwegian pastor to visit her.

Until now I had only heard her voice on the telephone, so this was our first meeting face to face. Expecting to see her as a typical prisoner without much concern about physical appearance, I was struck immediately that she was well groomed with makeup and that she had dressed beautifully.

"I want you to have a good impression of me," she explained. She gave me a big hug as if we were old friends and thanked me for coming.

We had been given permission for a twenty-minute visit, but it stretched to two hours. We sat for a conversation filled with tears. For me, it was a very difficult experience hearing the genuine pain of a fellow human being. She confessed her sins, regretting the mistakes of the past.

"If you are allowed to live in freedom again," I asked, "how would you live? Would you ever think about doing the same act?"

Her response was straightforward without hesitation. She said, "I believe that arms do nothing. I would fight with the word. Nonviolence is the way." Here was a person who had been a freedom fighter, called a terrorist by many, and now she says that weapons accomplish nothing.

She also expressed her sorrow that she could not raise her child in Palestinian society and that Laila, now eleven years old, had to be raised by her father alone in Norway. She was feeling very bad after two hours of intense confession.

"As my priest, will you give me Holy Communion?" Suheila asked me.

However, I had not brought the elements along with me. The best I could do was promise to return. "When I am traveling next in Europe, I will return to give you Holy Communion."

The next time I was in Europe, I contacted her husband from whom I received a warm welcome. "I have come to give her Holy Communion." However, he announced that she would not see me. Only later would I learn that she had turned suicidal and had tried several times to take her life. The Norwegian press had been very critical of her: "What is this terrorist doing living in Norway?"

Some Norwegian individuals were also critical: "Why does this pastor visit her?"

For me as a called minister in the church of God, my pastoral role requires me to respond to human need wherever that may be. She was a human being who was hurting and in need of counseling. My actions were not intended to suggest sympathy with what she had done or to imply that I was in support of her violent past. Didn't Martin Luther often speak of loving the sinner while hating the sin. That certainly was the stance of Jesus in embracing the woman caught in adultery and in engaging in the practice of dining with "sinners." As I continued to visit her, I wondered how Ananias must have felt as he brought a ministry of healing and forgiveness to the one who had breathed threats and murder upon the early church—the man named Paul.

Yes, Norwegians were divided over her case. The ultraright demanded that her punishment continue. The left saw things differently. Encouragement came even from Sylvia Rafael, the former Israeli Mossad agent. This woman alone was offering support. "Don't give up," she wrote Suheila, and encouraged her to persevere.

When Suheila was extradited to Germany and imprisoned in Hamburg, she was kept under high security. Only the Norwegian Pastor Svein Raddum was allowed to visit her and he kept in close touch with me.

When Suheila was brought to trial, she said that she felt totally alone and continued to attempt suicide. Even her husband became so depressed that he, too, tried to kill himself. Suheila did not contest the charges. She admitted freely what she had done. After serving two years of her twelve-year sentence, she was moved to Norway because her psychological and physical health had deteriorated. In Oslo, she had further surgery on her knees and then was sent to a Norwegian prison to complete her term. All the time, I kept in contact with the pastor by phone and continued to discuss her progress and also was able to remain in contact with her husband. They felt hopeful that the Norwegians would be more open to my role in ministering to her in prison.

Some time passed, and Prime Minister Kjell-Magne Bundevik of Norway visited Palestine and Israel in 1999 with a stop in Beit Sahour. While there, he asked to have a private audience for about twenty minutes with me, now as the Lutheran bishop, without security. Since we knew each other from previous meetings and visits, he wanted to discuss several issues about the status of the Palestinian church. At the end of the discussion, I thought, "Now is the time to act." I got up the courage and asked, "What about Suheila Andrawes? I am her spiritual counselor, and through her local Norwegian pastor, I am remaining in close contact counseling her. I am thankful that you have allowed me to visit her in prison. She has suffered greatly. She is a changed person. This is the second time she has been imprisoned for this one crime. Can I appeal for her release?"

The prime minister responded, "I give you my word that I will look into this matter. I will speak with the minister of justice."

That was the end of the conversation, and then nothing. We waited. Four months later, I received a phone call, "Bishop Munib, I have been let out of prison. You are my bishop. I love you." Now, that is very unusual for an Arab woman to say to any man, "I love you." But it demonstrates her change of heart and the depth of her feelings. She saw me as her spiritual father who had helped to release her, not just from prison, but from this heavy burden of her past. How to compare it? Maybe to the sinful woman who came to Jesus with perfume and kissed his feet. That is the reaction of forgiveness. We were both so happy and rejoiced over her good fortune.

The matter was still far from finished. In January 2000, I was in Norway for meetings to celebrate the Jubilee. How significant! The whole purpose of the Jubilee was to focus on the meaning of forgiveness and rebirth. I was to discover, however, that Suheila had still not returned home to a normal life with her husband and daughter, but she was living in a rehabilitation center for mentally disturbed persons. Her ordeal with the German and Norwegian legal systems had resurrected all the feelings of guilt from her past. Pastor Raddum informed me that she refused now even his visits. She was filled with guilt. She could not face anyone. She had gone out from the center only once for two hours when she went to her home for Christmas. She would have been allowed more, but she simply could not stand to be with others—even her husband and daughter. So, she had asked to be taken back to the rehabilitation center.

I telephoned her husband. "I want to speak with Suheila."

He answered that he would try.

Then I announced, "I am coming with Holy Communion. Please inform her that I am coming. This is not a request. You are to instruct her that I am coming to give her Holy Communion, and she cannot say no."

When her husband and I arrived at the rehabilitation center, she greeted us with hugs and tears for nearly ten minutes. Once again, she had dressed beautifully and was well groomed. After this initial period, she asked to talk alone with me, so her husband left the room. Again I counseled her, hearing her speak of her shame and her fears. Finally, I responded, "You have paid your debt to society. With regard to the government, they agree that after years of imprisonment you are free. With regard to God, you know that the Lord promised forgiveness to those who repent. It is up to you to accept that as a gift. It is time to reconstruct your life with your husband. Your fifteen-year-old daughter Laila needs you."

We continued to talk. Then, I announced, "You have suffered for so long, but you are no longer in prison. It is not right that you continue to suffer in this way and be afraid to go out into society. You must face it. You made a mistake. But you have confessed. Now you must construct a normal life with your husband."

"But I can't," she begged me.

I responded, "You can take your time, but you must go to your husband. I am not coming back to this center to visit you. Take your time. You can prepare yourself for this on your own schedule. But next time, I will visit you in your own home. And you must prepare dinner for me—not your husband cooking, as he has been all these years—but you must prepare a meal yourself."

She responded that she would try her best. "Only one condition," she asked. "Please don't ask me to stop smoking." She had turned into a chain-smoker, and I was always asking her not to smoke in my presence.

"Never mind," I told her. "That's not important."

At that moment, I called her husband back into the room and announced, "I think we are ready for Holy Communion."

"Yes," she responded, but she asked if it were possible to sit because standing for a long time was painful for her. In spite of the repeated surgery, her knees still tormented her with pain. So she and her husband sat together and received Holy Communion. As they received the bread and wine, they were crying and hugging each other in a full outpouring of emotion. The absolution had finally become real for her: "May this body and blood of our Lord Jesus strengthen and preserve you."

After a little bit, I reported that it was time for my departure. "I will walk with you outside to the taxi," she announced. This was significant. Other than her brief trip home at Christmas, she had not allowed herself to leave the building and to go outside. Her shame had left her.

Nine months passed. It was September 2000, at the beginning of the new Intifada, when the telephone rang. "Bishop Munib, I am home. I am now living a normal life with my husband and daughter in Grefsen. However, I am now worried about you and the Palestinian people with this new Intifada beginning."

It had taken her nine months to return home, but it was finally complete. She then invited me to come to dinner at her home the next time I traveled to Norway. For the next several months, Suheila and Ahmad telephoned me frequently.

The promised dinner took place in January 2001, when I returned to Norway. Suheila took pride that everything was special. She had prepared everything herself, even baking her own bread. At the end of the evening, I again had the opportunity to share Holy Communion with the family.

Suheila has now been restored to her family. She has a loving relationship with her husband, who stood by her patiently all these years. She now is helping to raise her daughter Laila, who had been without a mother for so long. She is healthy except for her knees, and she remains a chain-smoker. The family attends church regularly, and the congregation in Grefsen has accepted them fully.

When I reflect on my role in this story, I can only say, "I did nothing special, but to be a pastor with a human being in need. I was fulfilling the biblical *martyria*—being a witness—without knowing." As a witness, my effort had its risks.

Suheila's own message is clear, that she will follow the path of non-violence. "The tongue is always stronger than the bullet," she declares. "I will always fight injustice with the word of my mouth." Suheila Andrawes, too, has been transformed into a witness for peace.

9

Principles for Witness
in Theological Trialogue

When I was elected bishop, one of my Palestinian friends presented
me a gift, an oil painting of a rabbi, a priest, and an imam (a Muslim cleric) engaged in trialogue.[1] I was delighted to see how well this
friend had grasped my theology. While I admired the masterpiece, I was
also forced to confront some difficult questions.

First, I observed the costumes of the three participants. They were
truly from an age gone by. I wondered, is trialogue a thing of the past?
Can the good relationships that existed among the three monotheistic
religions in Palestine prior to 1948 be revived? Are there any real chances
for fruitful trialogue as we enter the third millennium?

Next, I observed that the participants were all men, all clergy, all
elders in their respective communities. I thought about participants in
today's trialogue: Will they be only the clergy and the elderly? Will the
voices of women, of the young, of the laity be heard? Can we make the
issue of trialogue appealing to the young, as I believe we must if trialogue is to be successful?

The first formal trialogue in which I participated took place in
Sweden, before the signing of the Oslo Accords. At that time, such an
effort seemed doomed to failure, since we had not met in constructive
trialogue for so many decades. Tensions ran high, and participants were
not ashamed to expose their fears and prejudices. But the process, while
difficult, was a worthwhile one of growing together and achieving a
spiritual revival. It awakened in us the desire for further trialogue through
which we could build mutual trust and eventually recognize and accept
each other's differences.

Thus, I am optimistic about trialogue in the twenty-first century. At the same time, however, I do not believe that trialogue is like fast food or instant coffee or any other commercial commodity. It cannot provide instant rewards. Rather, it is like a school where ideas are explored and understood gradually, and difficulties are overcome one by one, as they arise.

Essential Requirements for Constructive Trialogue

I believe trialogue can be fruitful only if the following conditions are met:

- Reality must be accepted. We must not speak of utopian solutions or cling to unrealistic expectations. We must realize that our hopes and efforts are always restricted by reality's limits. Accepting and defining reality means acknowledging existing diversity while recognizing real opportunities for coming closer together.
- Issues should be discussed one at a time. We should not attempt to solve all the world's religious and political problems at once; rather, we must concentrate on individual subjects and discuss them as thoroughly as possible.
- Absolute claims should be avoided. If we insist on viewing every issue only from our own viewpoint, from within our own religious tower, we will never understand the legitimate position of the other. Trialogue means overcoming egocentric individualism and discovering the marvelous diversity of God's world.
- The "otherness" of the other must be respected. Once we realize that we are dealing with real people, not stereotypes or caricatures of one another, we can develop the mutual respect that is essential for successful trialogue. Such respect means neither immediate approval nor blind acceptance. Rather, it means that all sides enter the trialogue with the assumption that they will be treated with respect and with the willingness to accord that respect to others.
- God's spirit should be present in trialogue. Trialogue is not an intellectual exercise; it must have a spiritual and symbolic dimension in order to be deep and enduring. We must submit ourselves to God's will so that God may help us to be self-critical, while at the same time transforming us, so that we can find the path toward a just present and a secure future.

The Functions of Trialogue

There are those who see trialogue as an intellectual exercise that makes everyone feel good but has no impact on real life. I disagree. I believe trialogue fulfills two essential functions with the potential to transform our lives.

It has a priestly function. The Bible makes it clear that religion's role is to cultivate communities of people who are spiritually mature and responsible. In fact, caring for people's spiritual life has always been of utmost importance in the history of all religions. In the modern world, however, religion has lost ground in the spiritual realm. Secularism, atheism, and indifference to religion, as well as narrow religious fundamentalism, have pushed religion aside. What room is there, then, for trialogue to play a priestly role in such a world?

Walter Brueggemann presents an interesting perspective on the role of authority in church education.[2] He notes that the authority of God served as the starting point for education in ancient Israel. Thus, he contends, religious instruction must be based on well-established, recognized authority. The problem today, according to Brueggemann, is that the church has lost its authority and become "Torah-less." I believe that trialogue, in its priestly function, can help restore religion to its rightful place as a strong and positive spiritual authority. Rather than a meaningless intellectual exercise, trialogue can help members of all three religions to develop and nurture the spiritual dimension in their lives.

I myself have experienced this spiritual awakening through trialogue. Whenever I am asked by members of my church what benefits I reap from trialogue, aside from just talking, I answer that I have undergone significant spiritual growth, as I have rediscovered God in myself and in others.

Trialogue also has a prophetic function. Responsible religion cannot be static. It is dynamic—always moving forward to promote God's will, to bring justice, and to encourage new ways of thinking.

The biblical prophets were unpopular because they spoke up against institutions that abused religion and perverted justice, proclaiming God's will. Listen to the words of the prophet Amos, for example, who said, "Take away from me the noise of your songs; I will not listen to the melody of your harps. But let justice roll down like waters, and righteousness like an ever-flowing stream" (Amos 5:23-24). Didn't Jeremiah suffer, as he uttered powerful and painful oracles against his own people? And didn't Jesus Christ suffer to the cross, as he challenged the religious and social institutions of his time?

If trialogue is to be effective and inspirational, it must assume the prophetic role of addressing social injustice. It must apply God's standards of justice to contemporary issues, seeking to right wrongs and promote human rights.

So, trialogue cannot be an exercise of talking to ourselves, but it should be an opportunity to promote justice and refrain from any kind of egoism. If trialogue is to be effective and inspirational, it should activate a paradigm shift in the thinking of the adherents and address the social injustice that is prevailing. The trialogue cannot live in isolation from the world, refusing to adopt a prophetic role that addresses the contemporary issues from God's perspective, a perspective of justice. "Justice, and only justice" is the mother of trialogue. The prophetic role of the trialogue is to support freedom of religion, human rights, and social justice. The credibility of such a trialogue depends on its prophetic proclamation of justice in a broken world.

Trialogue as a Catalyst for Reconciliation

As our peoples stand at this junction in history, we must look at our religions critically, and ask ourselves: Have they been a source of conflict and disagreement or a basis for reconciliation? Have they built bridges or have they widened the gap between the peoples of this country? It is so easy to blame others and not examine ourselves. It is also easy to blame the other's religion without examining our own. It is so tempting in this region to use religion for narrow, selfish purposes—especially for political interests.

The real conflict between Palestinians and Israelis is over land, yet it is often turned into a religious issue. Thus, sublime religion is converted to political ideology. Religion loses its essence of caring for all human beings and becomes merely a tool to implement a narrow ideological program. In the 1970s, I used to read the apocalyptic literature dealing with the Cold War relationship between the United States and the Soviet Union. I saw how religion bred hatred, and I asked myself whether these theologians saw God as anything more than a rationalization of their ideologies. I was also reminded of tribal battles described in the Old Testament, in which each tribe's gods were supposed to care only for that tribe's interests. And I wonder, do we—Jews, Christians, and Muslims—still adhere to this tribal mentality?

As we enter the third millennium, we must search our souls and evaluate ourselves. Have we been serving God and humanity, or merely our own narrow self-interests? And we must kneel together and ask for God's forgiveness. We must ask, "What do you, Lord Almighty, want us to do?" And we must be responsive with the prophet Samuel: "Speak, LORD, for your servant is listening."

We are called to hear God's voice and to serve as catalysts of reconciliation in our highly volatile region. We are called to seek the values that are common to the three monotheistic religious, to pray together, to engage in dialogue with one another, to recognize each other's human, national, political, and religious rights. We must do all these things for the future of two nations in a shared land. The synagogue, the church, and the mosque must cultivate a new culture of love in this Holy Land. That is God's call for the third millennium.

No implementation of a peaceful settlement will take place unless the people are reconciled. Some ask us, "Do we have to reconcile now or after the entire peace treaty between our government is signed?" I am well aware that the conflict needs a political and just settlement for peace. However, peace will not emerge by a mere handshake of the leaders or by their signing of peace accords, but people at the grass roots need to be reconciled. They still see each other only as enemies. Walls of animosity and divisiveness are still being erected between our two peoples. Stigmatizations, prejudices, demonization of the other, and violence are still the common language. After the Oslo and Wye agreements, did the situation really change? How can our peoples alter their images of the other and thereby change their animosity into neighborliness, oppression into equality, insecurity into security, and hatred into love?

Here comes the prophetic role of trialogue. The three monotheistic religions need to find courageous ways and means to break the shackles of the vicious cycle of hatred and even to challenge the political structures. Trialogue should be a catalyst that looks at reality in an objective way and transforms the people for mutual recognition and the acceptance of each other's human, national, civil, political, and religious rights.

We know that the process of reconciliation may be long and painful. When two rivers merge into one, they flow a long distance before their separate currents are reconciled. But it is feasible, if we believe in a living, reconciling God who can make the seemingly impossible possible.

Promoting Peace Education through Trialogue

In promoting reconciliation, trialogue must serve as a model for tolerance and lay the groundwork for a new approach to education. Positive attitudes toward the other must be fostered, not for the purposes of political strategy, but for the sake of real mutual acceptance. As in seventeenth-century Europe, when the term *tolerance* was first used in the context of religious conflict, its definition should be the one from Galatians 6:2: "Bear one another's burdens."

Tolerance does not mean putting up with everything, but rather accepting and welcoming diversity and realizing that society benefits from a multiplicity of lifestyles and ideas. These points must be emphasized in the peace education promoted by trialogue.

And now is the time for promoting such peace education. Although all of us in this region carry the scars of our stormy past, we must, through peace education, liberate our minds and memories and adopt a new concept of reality. Israeli children are taught that their security is in weapons. Palestinian children know only the Israeli who kills, confiscates their land, detains their fathers, and prevents their parents from entering Jerusalem to earn a living. Both sides must be liberated from these notions and taught that real security will only come through reconciliation with their neighbors.

Someone once told me that the Israelis are a nation under siege, and that is what colors their behavior. Similarly, Palestinians are a nation under occupation, and that shapes the way they behave. Ugly pictures of one another are perpetuated by family, the media, the curricula in schools, and society at large. How can we break the vicious cycle? Through peace education, based on tolerance, equality, and forgiveness.

To achieve the goals of peace education, trialogue must operate in several areas. It must

- work for change in the school curricula of both nations, so that national and religious triumphalism are excluded, and mutual tolerance is promoted. The demonizing of the other must end, and an objective reading of history must be sought.
- encourage education about the three monotheistic religions, as they see themselves. This means we are to avoid narrow interpretations

or comparative teachings or wrong generalizations. Children should be taught to view other religions positively and realistically and to approach one another with love.

- promote exchanges among clergy, lay adults, youth, and children to break down stereotypes at a grassroots level. They need to share the painful and joyful experiences and to encourage each side to see the human in the other, paving the way to a just peace.

These three points are not a political agenda for peace education, but they are the prophetic function of the trialogue. The synagogue, the church, and the mosque are the formative sites where attitudes are nurtured. Trialogue for peace education must always ask, "What is our common responsibility? Can we change attitudes? Can we live in a just peace after ten years or more? Can we share the land and still live together, allowing the others to implement their aspirations?" Peace education is the act of living together. It is based on the biblical verse: "Love your neighbor as yourself" (Leviticus 19:18; Luke 10:27).

The Global Impact of Trialogue

Hans Küng understood the formative role of religious dialogue: "There will be no peace among the peoples of this world without peace among the world religions." He goes on to talk about religious dialogue as the key to peace among religions.[3] I would add to his idea by saying, "There is no peace in the world unless religions properly assume their prophetic role and strive for social justice in the world." In an era of injustice, ethnic cleansing, discrimination, and religious fundamentalism, religion cannot remain silent. It must stand on the side of the weak and the powerless, serving as the conscience of society.

The three monotheistic religions have a common responsibility to seek social justice, not only in Palestine and Israel and the Middle East, but in the entire world. Like the biblical prophets, we must care not only for our own people but for all of humanity. We must use our shared biblical traditions to work for freedom, equality, and democracy everywhere. We must not lose sight of issues like the plight of the poor, those suffering from illness, care for the environment and all of God's creation. All too often, the conflict situation here has diverted our attention, so that we forget about these issues in a broader context.

In the name of our common God, it is our duty to create a world in which every individual enjoys dignity and respect. This is the imperative of trialogue: to work together until universal justice is realized.

I once saw graffiti in a London subway station that proclaimed: "The world is fragile; handle it with prayer." I would add: "Palestine/Israel is fragile. Handle it with prayer and reconciliation." This is our agenda of trialogue.

10

Witness to the Muslim Community

I grew up in the Old City. Although my home was located in the Christian Quarter, there were many Muslim merchants there with whom I had constant contact. For some Christians, the idea of dialogue with Muslims is foreign, and acting on it must be deliberately intended. For me, it is natural. My life has always been in the midst of Muslims. To some degree, my counsel when it comes to Muslim–Christian interaction is more practical than theological. Yet the two are intertwined.

Practical Relations

Shortly after I became bishop and moved into my office at the Lutheran Church of the Redeemer, several of the church windows were broken. The doorkeeper suspected the culprits had girls and wanted to go to the tower for privacy. When he tried to stop them, they gave him a good beating.

So the probst came to me. He was clearly upset, even shaking as he described what had happened.

"I can take care of it," I told him.

He responded as if I were a naive young bishop who didn't know anything. He thought that either I would be unable to handle it or I would hide it and do nothing. The probst responded in a Western way: "I'll go to the police." But I belong to the Arab society. I don't claim to be better than the Muslims. I can go to them.

I called some of my contacts and informed them of the situation. "Please find who did this. I'll give you twenty-four hours to find them." Sometimes, Muslims respect us more when we go directly to them.

Then, my contacts came to my office. "Oh, Bishop Munib," they said. "We are very sorry. We know who did this. Please understand, it was not meant for you."

"I know it is not a Muslim–Christian issue," I responded. "It was vandalism, but the man who attacks the house of God must be punished. We cannot tolerate that." This was my argument. I knew it was not a Muslim–Christian problem. I grew up here and I know better. Whoever they are, they must show respect for the house of God in the same way as we respect a mosque. So they must be punished.

They said, "We'll bring them here to you, and then they'll apologize."

"No, I won't accept that," I responded. "Have their fathers and uncles come, and I will discuss it with them."

They agreed.

Then I went on, "Don't you ever think you can make it a Muslim–Christian fight here in Jerusalem. No one will succeed—not you, or your children, or your children's children. I grew up in Jerusalem. I know the people. I can walk here in the streets. When someone does wrong, who defends me? Not the Christians, but my Muslim friends. My daughter Anna—back when there was a dispute with the settlers over the St. John's hostel—she was five or six and was crying in the street, a Muslim shopkeeper saw her and brought her into his shop. He gave her ice cream and told her to wait while he found her father. I asked him, 'Why?' His answer: 'Because we know you. You are one of us.'"

So I requested that good people from the town come and apologize. Why? Not because I want to punish them, but because I want to teach that nobody should think they can intervene between Muslims and Christians and create a friction between them. Now, the probst had thought I would sweep this under the carpet. No, I handled it, but in a different way than he could because I knew the people. They would think he was preaching to them.

What happened? Fifty merchants from Jerusalem came and apologized. And it wasn't easy.

They said, "Oh, bishop, what are you doing? We are brothers."

I replied, "Yes, we are brothers. But the one who attacks the house of God must be punished."

"Oh, we will forgive them. You know the families are poor," they said, thinking of compensation.

So we had our meeting. They apologized. I forgave them. In the process, we talked about our two communities, about the need to respect each other and our houses of worship. The problem was settled, and it did not develop into a Muslim–Christian conflict.

Now, the probst comes to me when there are problems. "You are one of them," he says. But still, it is never easy. It is sometimes very complicated, and we have to be patient. They know our intentions are good. But we never allow it to become a crisis. If I had ignored the issue, there would have been talking, charges, and countercharges. It could easily have developed into a Muslim–Christian crisis in the town. It would have been like fire in dry grass.

When I think about Muslim–Christian relations, I consider how practical they are, not how official. I want to teach a Western audience a paradigm of living. I don't know how I can express it sometimes. I have to face it every day. Yesterday, we were walking together as a family in the street and came upon a young boy playing. He joked with me: "I want to marry, I want to marry." He's not a member of my congregation. He's a Muslim. His father and I used to play marbles. We grew up together. Now, this is how national identity evolves. If it blows up, we face it in the streets. If it prospers, we prosper together. This brings me to good relations. One of our congregational members had a small financial problem the other day. I didn't even think about calling a church council member. I called a local merchant, quite elderly and affluent. He solved it. He is a Muslim.

There are several important lessons for the Christian church wherever we are.

First of all, it is important that we not overlook practical issues. We are to be concerned as servants, not to approach the situation as masters.

Second, it is very important not to sow seeds of conflict with the Muslim community, but to enter into constructive dialogue.

Third, it is important to be in solidarity with them in times of crisis and sorrow. For example, their funerals are crucial events. If there is a death, you go. If you don't go to their weddings, they don't care. But if you don't go to their funerals, they hold it against you. In the West, when you are invited to a wedding and you don't go, it is an insult. When there is a funeral, you think, "Oh, I shouldn't disturb the family. I'll leave them alone." But here, it's different. When Muslims go to pay condolences, they go in families, a crowd of families, fifty or sixty men walking together in the streets.

These three practical elements are important for the church here. When I show these three examples, we can coexist together.

Attitudes among the Laity

All Palestinian Christians certainly do not have the same attitudes toward relationships with Muslims. Some are conditioned by where they were brought up and where they live. Others are influenced by religious fundamentalism, both in Christianity and in Islam.

One group strongly supports pan-Arabism. They focus on the whole cultural and national life and believe that Muslim–Christian cooperation is essential. They think that we should deal with problems and mistakes as Palestinians, not transfer the political conflict with Israel to a religious one among ourselves. This group is by far the majority, including Christians and many Muslim sheiks.

The second group is simplistic. We have some difficulties with them, because they judge every incident in black and white. "You like the Muslims. Look what they have done to us Christians." Some people on both sides identify only with their own group. "Because they are Christians, we have to deal differently with them." And we are afraid, because the simplistic people are numerous. There are also opportunists among them. They are mercenaries.

This trend of Muslim–Christian tension is recent. The younger generation is more susceptible to it than the older people who grew up together. Our challenge is how we can pursue cooperation in future generations in the right way. We do it in Christian schools. With the weakening of ideologies and of pan-Arabism, we are anxious about how this will work out. Those who have lived together know there is another identity, a common identity.

When Christian villages nearest Jerusalem—Beit Jala and Beit Sahour—were being shelled by Israelis for being Palestinian bases during the opening months of the al-Aqsa Intifada, the community of Bethlehem, a city with a Christian minority, raised a number of questions. Some were saying, "Look, the Muslims want the Christians to be killed." When the American church leaders' delegation came, they, too, raised the question, "Are the Muslims shooting from these villages because they want Israel to retaliate against the Christians?" The facts about the strategic locations and the logic of other situations do not support these suspicions. Why didn't we come to the same conclusion in Rafah in

Gaza? Why did we not say that attacks were made from there because shooters wanted members of a Muslim community killed? The logic breaks down. This disturbs me.

The next Sunday when I preached in Beit Sahour, I refuted such statements: "Don't you think when we respond as Christians in this way, we are inviting Islamic fundamentalism? You cannot answer fanaticism with another's fanaticism or you are the loser. You are only a winner by increasing a common nationalism." The congregation in Beit Sahour appreciated that sermon. I could see it.

The Gifts of Islam

During this tense time in Middle Eastern politics—both in the Palestinian-Israeli conflict and in the war on terrorism, which focuses on individuals who have perverted their own religion—it is important to get at the heart of Islam. What do the vast majority of Muslims believe?

The linguistic connections between the name Islam and the Arabic word for peace, *salaam,* are instructive. The goal of Islam is to build a household of peace—as in the city name *Dar es Salaam.* The common greeting of Muslims everywhere is not hello or good-bye, but *Assalaamu-aleikum*—peace be with you. Peace is established not by dominance, but by submission—the literal meaning of the word *Islam.*

This submission is made evident in the Five Pillars: the confession of faith, prayer, charity, fasting, and pilgrimage. This is the heart of teaching about Islam.

The first pillar, the *shahada,* reminds the believer that there is one God, Allah, and that Muhammad is the ultimate prophet. Surprisingly, there are many in the world who assume that Muslims worship a different God than do Christians. Middle Eastern Christians know that this is not the case. Allah is simply the Arabic word for the one God worshiped by Muslims, Jews, and Christians. Linguistically, its roots are found in the Canaanite name for God, *El,* and it is related to the Hebrew word *Elohim,* translated "God" throughout the Old Testament. We share this common heritage. Palestinian Christians are aware of this commonality every time we read the New Testament in our Arabic translation, whenever we begin our worship with the phrase *bismallah* ("in the name of God"), or whenever in our daily conversation we say *anshallah* or *lahamdilla* ("God willing" or "thank God"). We are in total agreement. There is one God, Allah.

Christians, of course, place their emphasis on the role of Jesus, while Muslims confess Muhammad as the ultimate prophet. Many Westerners are unaware that Muslims do revere Jesus—*Isa* in Arabic—as a prophet. His mother Miriam (Mary) is the most frequently mentioned woman in the Qur'an, and the virgin birth is accepted. Christians do not reciprocate by expressing honor for Muhammad but often speak disparagingly about him. This seems to be more culturally biased than objective. There is no question of his contribution to the religious life of Muslims. He is considered to be the Arab prophet. One wonders whether God did not use Muhammad to speak an important message to the people of the Arabian peninsula.

Having said this, I am not so eager to delve into other doctrinal issues with Muslims, such as the nature of the Triune God, the divinity of Christ, or his salvific work through the cross. Here Muslims and Christians are at odds. Too often, Christians begin with these doctrinal issues, which lead only to theological discussion and disagreement. Such debates sidetrack us and derail any fruitful discussion. We must begin with the commonalities. By focusing on what we share, we can build trust and understanding.

To seek coexistence, we must recognize common values.

First, there is the value of respecting others as they are. The idea of loving the neighbor as yourself is found in the Qur'an, in the Torah, and, of course, in the New Testament.

Second, Muslims are concerned about justice. Islam can perhaps teach us more about material and secular justice. The Islamic laws, the *shariah,* give instructions for the right path of practical justice—for example, how to treat your wife, how to divide an inheritance—from A to Z. Justice is a commonality.

Third, the pillars of Islam place an emphasis on worshiping the living God. Christians may have something to learn from Jews and Muslims about the seriousness of worshiping.

The second pillar is fulfilled by devout Muslims submitting to God in prayer five times every day, a degree of piety difficult to find elsewhere. Devotion is evident when the muezzin calls out before the crack of dawn for individuals to rise for prayer. It is evident when Muslims in non–Middle Eastern countries learn the Arabic language to recite the *Fatiha* and the required *suras.* It is evident when Muslims prostrate themselves upon the ground as a sign of true submission to God. When

I interact with Muslim businessmen in the Old City, I see that calloused mark on their foreheads from years of sincere devotion in daily prayers.

While Muslim devotion is directed at submission to God, it is also directed outward toward neighbor. The third pillar, called *zakat,* calls upon Muslims to provide charity for those in need. The expectation is for donations of 2.5 percent of their income. In my experience, however, their generosity exceeds that figure. It is not unusual when someone in our church is in need for me to approach Muslim businessmen, who unhesitatingly make a contribution to someone they may not even know. We are living at a time of extreme economic hardship for the Palestinian people. It has been estimated that West Bank residents are living on two dollars a day. Under these conditions, it has been difficult to develop the stewardship of our church members. For our Muslim friends, it is not a question of voluntary giving but an obligation of their faith. Muslim generosity from throughout the world has provided for the needs of Palestinians during this time.

That same devotion is evident in the fourth pillar of fasting during the month of Ramadan. The discipline involves refraining from partaking of food, water, or any other substances during the daylight hours for the entire month—a powerful example of spiritual and bodily purification and cleansing. This is especially impressive in the Middle East in years when Ramadan falls during the hot summer months. In Jerusalem, the four Fridays of Ramadan draw Muslims to pray at al-Aqsa Mosque—many coming long distances and passing through Israeli checkpoints and obstacles. Even with the closures, more than half a million may come for prayer. The city is so crowded then that it is not unusual for me to find Muslims kneeling in the streets near my church. They do not hesitate to pay five shekels for a normally priced two-shekel loaf of bread, because it was baked in the holy city of Jerusalem. In contrast, I am sometimes discouraged to see only small numbers of Christians in our churches, even during our feasts. I'm learning from Muslims. I'm learning how to worship seriously. I'm learning from their spirituality.

The fifth pillar in Islam is the *hajj,* the pilgrimage to Mecca. Again, this is not well appreciated by Western Christians, especially among Protestants, whose focus is on the spiritual journey apart from shrines and Holy Places. Eastern Christians and Catholics, on the other hand, have stressed the significance of the city of Jerusalem in assisting the spiritual journey. Muslims have this understanding. Once in every Muslim's lifetime, he or she is expected to make the pilgrimage to Mecca in the month of the Hajj. It is a time of introspection and devotion. It is a time to emphasize the unity of all by participants' wearing the simple white garb of the pilgrim. Pilgrims retrace the steps of the biblical Isma'il (Ishmael) and have their own share in the story of faith. We in Jerusalem experience the Hajj through individuals who commit themselves for the pilgrimage. Many of us can share stories of lives that were changed because of the experience. Likewise, it has often been the goal of Muslims worldwide to include Jerusalem in their itinerary after completing the trip to Mecca and Medina. Jerusalem's Dome of the Rock is generally considered the third-holiest site in Islam. For many, the visit to Jerusalem is extended to include a trip to the burial place of Ibrihim (Abraham) in Hebron, and often also a visit to the birthplace of the prophet Isa (Jesus) in Bethlehem. Current political conditions have obstructed this important practice in the Muslim faith.

When one examines the devotion manifest in these Five Pillars, one can only be impressed. Islam is a religion of peace.

Some people have suggested that there is a sixth pillar, that of jihad. Here one finds the greatest misunderstanding of all. Jihad is often translated simply as "holy war." Unfortunately, many non-Muslims ignore the Five Pillars, the devotion of submission, and the attitude of peace; they think of Islam as a religion of violence. Jihad, however, is properly translated as "striving" or "struggling." In a sense, then, the meaning is similar to the Hebrew root of the name Israel ("he who struggles with God"). The connotation of jihad is that submission to Allah is not passive. Rather, one actively strives to follow God's will.

Some interpret jihad in the context of extending Islam to others. Islam, like Christianity, is a missionary religion. As also in Christianity, there are different attitudes among adherents about how religion is to be promoted. There are many examples of exclusivist Christian missionary efforts and of exclusivist Christian attitudes toward non-Christians, of which we are not proud. As Christians, we would not like others to judge Christianity on the basis of the practices of a few. So also we should not judge Islam on the basis of exclusivist Muslims.

The Qur'an describes two kinds of jihad, the greater and the lesser jihad. The greater jihad is the internal striving by which an individual seeks to conquer evil with the forces of good. One strives with the mind, the tongue, and the hand to promote the positive aspects of Islam. The lesser jihad is sometimes translated as "holy war," but it means taking

up arms only in self-defense. For all practical purposes, the rules of this
lesser jihad are no different than those of the "just-war theory" advo-
cated first by Augustine and developed by Christian ethicists over the
centuries. War can be undertaken only under certain conditions: one
must first be attacked; one should not harm women, children, and the
innocent; harm is to be done only in proportion to harm received; one
is not to receive material gain; and true peace is the eventual goal of
the struggle.

The Christian Witness to Muslims

I think we can learn from each other. I do believe also, of course, that
we as Christians have a lot to give them.

One Christian gift is the theology of grace rather than retribution,
which seems stronger in Judaism and Islam. This is a basic truth for us.
Out of grace comes forgiveness. It seems that this is our witness in a
multireligious society. The challenge is: Do we Christians practice our
religion both among ourselves and toward others? Do we teach others
how to live in forgiveness and grace?

Another contribution is the theology of the cross. How are we to
be servants, not masters?

These values, if we can learn from each other, can aid us to live in
a just peace. No one will come forward and say mea culpa like Pope
John Paul. No Muslim will come. No Jew will come. But John Paul came
humbly and asked for forgiveness. That is a strength of Christianity.
The church needs to seek out opportunities where it can contribute
these qualities for peace and understanding in the whole Middle East.

Christian Openness to Muslims

Many ask how we can accept Islam and Judaism if we believe in Christ.
Didn't Jesus say, "I am the way, and the truth, and the life. No one
comes to the Father, except through me" (John 14:6)? Didn't Peter say,
"There is no other name under heaven...by which we must be saved"
(Acts 4:12)?

I believe that the New Testament and the Old Testament are contextual books. This does not mean that they are not our source of
teaching. But once one reads the context, one understands differently
than if it is taken out of the context and made into an absolute. If I

take only the words—way, truth, life—and ignore Jesus' life, I am not dealing fairly with the whole of Jesus' teaching. Jesus is still the way for me as a Christian. Without Jesus, I am nothing. I am to glorify no other name. I have no doubts. This is my solid faith.

At the same time, this solid faith does not require my exclusiveness. If I sit on the throne of judgment and try to fit people through a criterion to determine who is Christian and who is not, what is the difference between me and those who hold up the Qur'an or the Torah as a means to exclude people? There is a big difference between Jesus' example of inclusiveness and such a view.

Being open doesn't mean one is not a good Christian. But a good Christian cannot keep Christ closed in a box and live in fear that if the box is opened this Christ might flee. If Christ lives in me, he liberates me. He frees me to accept others who are different and to see Christ in the other and not only in myself.

Many of the narrowly pietistic think that if I do not accept this "no other way" teaching, I'm a heretic. No, I'm not a heretic, because I'm taking Christ seriously. We are also reminded of Peter's encounter with Cornelius in Acts 10. I don't hold Christ in my hand. Christ holds me in his hand. That is the difference. And once he holds me in his hand, then I am living according to his will. That is the intention of "coming to the Father through me." Christ went to the Father through the cross. He did not direct us to go through glory or to be judges for the world.

For example, Jesus spoke with Nicodemus (John 3). Although traditions may say so, the Bible never says directly that Nicodemus believed in Jesus. That did not stop Jesus from talking to him. They had a commonality. Jesus talked with the religious scribes, but he did not say to them, either you believe in me or you will go to hell. Rather, he said, everyone who believes in me will be saved. There's a difference. It does not mean that I have to behave like a judging Jesus or a judging God.

One has to be careful with these pietistic statements that give a rap to the conscience but at the same time do not answer the real needs of human beings. As a believer in Christ, I am under his grace and in his hands. I willingly do everything that he asks of me. But this never makes me exclusive or proud. It makes me inclusive to say, As God can save me, so God can save you. As God can show the way, we can show the way. Acts 10 demonstrates that people like Cornelius, who did not observe the Torah, really believed in God, perhaps better than we do.

I see a Muslim walking barefoot from Hebron—passing through all the checkpoints, humiliated, without food, starting at 4 o'clock in the morning—just to pray at 11:30 for half an hour at al-Aqsa Mosque. If he cannot find a place there, he prays in the street near my church. For heaven's sake, who am I to claim that this man is not a believer in God? I will just stand and open my mouth and say, "Lord, show me the truth." That's all I can say.

These ideas of inclusiveness are very important in our witness to fanatics. If I say, no, this praying Muslim is a sinner, I am filled with hypocrisy, and I myself need to repent. I don't know the whole truth. I know only part of the truth. I will know the whole Jesus when I go to heaven and see him face to face. For this reason, I am invited to be humble.

Another crucial question comes out of my study of Deutero-Isaiah. Why did the Old Testament already offer a universalistic view of faith? Why did the prophets say that God can save the Israelites and also the Egyptians and the Cushites (Isaiah 45:14)? One has to be not only very careful, but also very sensitive. A good Christian is sensitive to others. If you are indoctrinated to make Christianity into an ideology, then you are not sensitive to others. That really is the way of fanaticism.

To be a good Christian, I believe I must be careful to live the inclusiveness of the theology of grace and the theology of the cross. This is how I understand these texts.

Exclusiveness or inclusiveness are not the criteria for mission. Mission is witnessing to everyone I meet. This can be done in many ways. A narrow version of mission proclaims oneself and not Christ. Mission proclaims the kingdom of God on earth. I consider myself a missionary, but not a traditional missionary. I do not measure my success by how many come to faith because of my work, as do those who report back to mission boards. But I am a missionary in my whole attitude, because when I am moved, I am moved by my faith in Christ.

I am not aggressive toward others. Paul was not always aggressive in his approach, as in his sermon at the Areopagus in Athens (Acts 17:16-34). If he had taken an aggressive approach, he would have been killed. His approach was to teach people. He stood up and discussed the living God.

Today, one of the problems with mission work is that it is either word of God or converting people. Either... or. Even a narrow-minded missionary is always talking about Christ. A missionary approach should be inclusive—proclaiming the word, proclaiming God's kingdom on earth. God's kingdom means justice. God's kingdom means encountering other religions. God's kingdom means creating a better life on this earth. In this sense, I am a missionary in the depths of my bones.

Evangelism is related to spiritual revival in the church, although spiritual revival is very different today from the movements of Zinzendorf and Wesley in the 1700s. We can learn from them but cannot extend their methods to the present time or the local place. The New Testament approach was inclusive, and it has continued until now by planting churches and touching the hearts of many. The exclusive approach is a short-term one. It emphasizes baptism and confessing—"Oh, I believe that Christ is my personal Lord and Savior"—and counting the number of believers. The inclusive approach may not have such dramatic results, but its efforts, more difficult and demanding, will last over a long time. Who can claim that I do not speak about Christ? I approach the Muslims and Jews in my own way. Maybe they don't ask for baptism. Maybe they don't ask to join the church. But who can say that they aren't learning from my way of life or that my work has not made them different?

Catholic theology interprets Romans 2 as an inclusive approach, that everybody can be saved. I accept that. Perhaps Catholics are more practical in their theology than we are. We Lutherans need to find ways to serve as missionaries in the total meaning of the word, not just in theological debates about the cross. The church works in many ways through many people. The church cannot have only diaconia, or only mission, or only proclamation of the gospel, or only *martyria*. The word church—*ecclesia*—is inclusive: diaconia, mission, *martyria*, proclamation, dialogue, social justice. A Christian may be called to do any of them. For me, mission in the church is holistic. You don't just listen to the heart of one believer; you hear the hearts of all believers.

Many movements challenge me, such as the revival movement in Finland. I think the Finnish movement was good in Finland, but it may not be appropriate in Sweden or Russia, because it is directed to the real needs of the Finnish people. Revival has to be contextual. Even the Augsburg Confession must be seen as a contextual document. It was good for Germany in the sixteenth century. I translated it from German into Arabic for adoption in Palestine. Who cares about the last seven or eight articles if it presents a basic truth? But it is primarily contextual for Germany. We really need a new confession that speaks to the whole world. Melanchthon and Luther never saw Jesus as narrow. He was as wide as his arms could extend, as far as Jerusalem. How does Christ extend in this context? It is very basic. If I speak about justice issues, it is because Christ does not accept injustice. Concern for justice derives from the theology of the cross and Jesus' life.

Arab Christians have a history of working effectively within Islamic contexts. When General Khalid gained control of Egypt in the first generation of Islamic expansion, he did not destroy everything. He applied standards from the Qur'an to evaluate the compatibility of other religious writings before keeping or burning them. When Muslims began to discover the potential contributions of Hellenistic culture in the works of Aristotle, Plato, and the many Greek writings that had been lost to the West, they translated and preserved them. Arab Christians played a major role in building Arab culture through medicine, mathematics, algebra, and sciences. Arab Christians also helped Muslims to build a culture that was inclusive of other "people of the book." And the Arab Christians fostered the dialogue between Christian and Muslim theologians, especially in the seventh and eighth centuries. Many of the arguments used to illustrate the Trinity—for example, the sun's aspects of light, heat, and rays—were developed by Arab Christians. With this history in mind, we may be more optimistic about our role in the modern contexts, while we remain true to our Christian heritage.

The Model of St. Francis

The witness of Christians to Muslims must be one of service in a spirit of humility. We can take St. Francis as a model. Even the Turkish sultan was impressed to see such a person standing barefoot and in a simple brown robe before him. Of course, Francis is an example of humility, a prophet of his times. His prayer is really a missionary prayer, reflecting the way of *martyria* as the crusaders did not.

Among the missionaries in Palestine, there are two types: some who came in the last century whom no one remembers, and others who were very dearly loved. Since the establishment of the joint bishopric, what bishops are remembered? Many bishops were working to create a place through ecclesiastical structure. But we recall those who served, like Bishop Samuel Gobat who built schools and hospitals. People speak of Bishop Theodor Schneller with emotion because he understood what the Palestinians needed, and he answered them with his school and orphanage. Schneller is remembered as a servant.

Schneller is memorable as a Christian example for bringing twelve survivors of the massacre by the Druze in Lebanon to open the section for boarding students in 1860. From the beginning, the school educated Muslim students. Of course, there was a different attitude toward them then. By the time they finished school, they were good evangelicals.

Saint Francis is said to have advised, "Preach the gospel wherever you go. If necessary use words." The Lutheran church in Jerusalem has followed that model of service by building hospitals and schools. Since 1950, our Augusta Victoria Hospital has focused on the plight of Palestinian refugees. What an amazing witness the hospital has been to all the people it has served, but especially to the many Muslims.

It is important that this kind of ministry continue today, especially in times of crisis. The church needs to be concerned for the suffering of the Palestinian people as human beings in need. It does not matter what their religion is. When a person is hungry, we feed her. When a person is grieving, we comfort him. We do it because these are people created in the image of God.

Once I was visiting one of our church members at Augusta Victoria Hospital in Jerusalem. I noticed an eight-year-old Muslim girl who was a patient surrounded by her mother and several other women relatives, all showing worried and apprehensive looks.

I paused to say a few words of concern.

The mother noticed my cross and clerical collar. "You are a Christian bishop," she said.

"Yes."

"I think God hears your prayers," she continued. "Would you pray for my daughter?"

"Yes, of course."

While I was standing there over the bed of the child praying, the other women relatives were engaged in conversation behind my back.

"No, God doesn't hear his prayers."

"Yes, God hears his prayers. My daughter will get better. I'm sure of it!"

I continued to pray, trying not to be distracted. When I finished, the mother thanked me. The other women stood silent to the side. It didn't matter whether or not they were convinced. What mattered was that I had responded to this young girl's suffering and to her mother's request.

This is our calling as Christians. We are called to be witnesses on behalf of all who are suffering.

11

Witness to the
Jewish Community

In the spring 1991, just after the Gulf War and before the Oslo Accords, our family was invited to the home of Rabbi Naomi Kelman in Mamilla, the section of Jerusalem just west of the Old City. This was the first attempt at social engagement between Jewish rabbis and Christian pastors within our own homes. The goal was to celebrate Shabbat, seders, and Christian holidays together as a way of breaking down barriers and building up friendships.

Our children Anna and Andria were then ten and eight years old. Martha was just a small baby. All week Suad and I prepared our children on proper etiquette and rules of behavior for the occasion. "Please behave. We must do nothing to offend them." "Please don't mention any of the comments you might have heard on the playground." "Please don't say, 'You Jews....'" On and on, we drilled our children as if any mistakes might lead to an international incident.

When we arrived at their home, we all sat quietly in the living room trying to force polite conversation. Rabbi Kelman and I had previously participated in formal religious dialogue, but our families had never met. It seemed as though everyone was wondering if this meeting on a social level was such a good idea after all. The room was filled with tension.

"Wouldn't your children like to play?" Rabbi Kelman asked.

"No, ma'am," our children replied, as they sat perfectly still in their chairs with their hands folded properly on their laps. "Thank you, we are just fine."

Suad and I both thought to ourselves that we had coached them well. We should be proud of our children. They were demonstrating that Palestinian children do understand proper manners. Yet, we also knew that this was very awkward and that we had a long evening ahead of us.

Eventually, something happened—I don't remember precisely—but the Kelman children invited Anna and Andria to see their rooms. From that point, we as parents began to relax and to engage in real conversation. The evening flew by. We adults were laughing and enjoying each other's company as if we were neighbors.

But what about the children? We had totally forgotten them. Off in the children's rooms, they were having a wonderful time. "Oh please, Papa, do we have to go home already?"

What a relief! Naomi turned to Suad: "We were so worried about our children's behavior. I have been coaching them all week on what to say and what not to say."

"So have we!" Suad revealed that we had been doing the very same thing and how anxious we were about our children's behavior.

The evening was a success. Both families had become better acquainted on a very human level. Later, the Kelmans came for an evening in Ramallah, not as occupiers but as true friends. They in turn invited us back for seders and Shabbat meals. We learned so much from the process about each other's religion, and misunderstandings were cleared up. Even more important is the real friendship we have developed now over the years. Through Naomi I have also gotten to know her brother, Rabbi Levi Kelman.

Our children have grown up together. They have seen each other socially, and they telephone each other all the time. They used to discuss becoming involved in the peace movement together. My daughter Anna is now a university student in Bethlehem. Rabbi Levi Kelman's daughter now serves in the Israeli Defense Forces, stationed at Rafah in Gaza. Her military service, required of young Israeli women and men, was very difficult for me. I didn't like to think of her in uniform, representing the occupation. Yet, she is still a person dear to me.

During the early months of the al-Aqsa Intifada, nine or ten Israeli soldiers were killed while standing at a bus stop on the road to Gaza by a Palestinian driver. When I heard the news, I felt deep concern in my heart. Immediately, I picked up the phone to call Rabbi Kelman. "Please,

I just heard the news," I said. "Is your daughter all right?" She was fine. She had just telephoned home to say that she was still at her base in Rafah.

This is the dilemma. Officially, she is my "enemy." However, I am afraid for her as if she were my own daughter. I have learned to see God in other human beings, and they likewise. If I don't feel concern for them as human beings, then I have lost my own humanity.

The Gifts of Judaism

My Jewish dialogue partners have shared with me the story of Rabbi Hillel, who lived two thousand years ago, about the same time as Jesus. Reportedly, someone came up to him one day asking for a short synopsis of the Jewish faith. "Please, you must give me the basics while standing on only one foot," the inquirer announced. Apparently, he wished to limit this famous rabbi's time so that he would be informed only about the essentials.

Hillel supposedly replied, "Love God with your whole heart. Love your neighbor as yourself." This is the summary of Judaism.

What impresses me about this story is the parallel in Jesus' teaching. When a scribe asked him which is the greatest commandment, Jesus responded with exactly the same point on loving God and loving neighbor (Mark 12:28-34). This should not be surprising. After all, Jesus grew up in the heart of Judaism and taught as a Jewish rabbi with Jewish disciples. Both his words and those of Hillel about loving God are found in the Torah section known as the Shema (Deuteronomy 6:4), which is repeated in the daily prayers of Jews everywhere. Loving the neighbor is also a Torah command, from Leviticus 19:18.

Christians and Jews share these same Hebrew Scriptures and have developed as two branches of a tree with common roots. This is why, as a young man, I was fascinated with the Old Testament stories and determined to study Hebrew, so I could understand them from a Jewish perspective. This is also why I chose to write my dissertation in Finland on Deutero-Isaiah.

By focusing on the oneness of God, Jews have taught us the importance of creation and the gift of the world God has given to us. It is a world to be appreciated and to be taken care of, especially now as we face an ecological crisis. Shabbat is a reminder that we as humans need to understand the concept of rest. It balances the story of Adam and

Eve in the garden, whose desire for knowledge shows the human inclination to want to control the world and to have dominion in such a way that puts humans first. Shabbat, on the other hand, is a reminder to let God be God and to let go of controlling this world. It emphasizes love of God and love of neighbor.

My study has made me most appreciative of the Jewish concept of justice. Jewish biblical writers emphasized the image of God within humanity. The Ten Commandments apply divine law to all, regardless of social class, gender, or nationality. The persistent prophetic voices challenge the powerful and defend the widow, the orphan, and the alien. With good reason, the prophets' words are the most frequently quoted part of the Hebrew Scriptures in the New Testament.

Through my dialogues with Jewish rabbis, I have come to realize that they provide an important example for Middle Eastern Christians in their two-thousand-year history of minority status. Even in biblical times, their experience included occupation, oppression, and subjugation by Egyptians, Assyrians, Babylonians, and by the Romans when Christianity first emerged. The stories of their faithfulness under these situations must be held up and celebrated. Their quest for freedom and liberation still animates the Passover seder. Jews came to experience dispersion and emigration, yet they remained faithful. All of this can be instructive to us as Palestinian Christians.

It is sometimes tempting to ignore or neglect this last two thousand years of Jewish history as somehow irrelevant, or at least inferior to the Jewish history in the biblical record. One must not trivialize the consequences of a long history of anti-Semitism—permanent scars of fear and insecurity concerning their own place in society. How can one address the impact of the Holocaust? No Jewish family has been left untouched by this horrendous episode. It calls for sensitivity and respect on our part.

The political issue of land has worked to divide us. Yet, from a theological standpoint, we can see from the Jewish people how land serves as a spiritual blessing. It was evident from the years of dispersion when Jews spoke of Passover hope with "Next year in Jerusalem!" It is evident from the devotion and sincerity of Jews who pray daily at the Western Wall. It is evident from the efforts of American and European Jews who travel to Jerusalem for a family Bar Mitzvah. It is evident by the way in which Israeli fathers and mothers take pride in the land and teach their children the biblical stories in their historical context.

Christians are people of the New Testament. By virtue of this, they are sometimes inclined to emphasize the "Old" for Jews in terms of an incomplete, outmoded, or inadequate scripture. But when Marcion, a second-century Christian, tried to cut out the Old Testament from the Christian Bible, he was overruled. The covenant with Abraham and Moses remains and has been fulfilled in Christ. Paul, in Romans 9–11, has explained this relationship for us. We, as Gentile Christians, are the wild branch grafted onto the olive tree to bear fruit. As Krister Stendahl puts it, we have been named honorary Jews and children of the covenant.[1] As for the Jews, they remain children of the covenant according to the promises made to Abraham and Moses. This all takes place according to the mysteries of God—which is something that those of us who live by grace can readily affirm.

Taking the name Israel from the patriarch Jacob who wrestled with God in Genesis 32, Jews are not afraid to struggle with deep theological issues. This has been the heritage of the rabbinic traditions included in the Mishnah, the Talmud, and subsequent commentaries. When it comes to our theological dialogues, it is especially encouraging that we begin and end according to Jewish custom with the word *shalom* and the Arabic *salaam*. Our dialogues can be challenging, but they take place in the spirit of peace. They are not carried out merely as an intellectual exercise or as a quest to demonstrate superiority. The goal on both sides is to love God with our whole heart and to love our neighbor as ourselves.

The Absence of Dialogue

The story of Jewish–Christian interaction in the Holy Land is completely different from that of Christian–Muslim contact. Unlike the Arab–Christian experience of living side by side with Arab Muslims our entire lives, we and Israelis have for the most part been forced to live a separate existence.

My own experience is illustrative of this situation. Through all my years growing up, I had no contacts with Jews. For nineteen years, from 1948 to 1967, no Jews lived in the Old City, which was part of the West Bank of the Kingdom of Jordan. The state of Israel, including West Jerusalem, was separated from the Old City and the West Bank by a no-man's-land and strict borders. Soon after Israel's occupation of the Old City, I went to study in Finland for seven years. By the time I returned to active ministry in Jerusalem, Beit Jala, and Ramallah, there were no opportunities for interaction.

On the other hand, with new ecumenical study centers arising throughout Jerusalem, such as Tantur, expatriate Christians were beginning to engage in theological dialogue with Jewish counterparts. Their interest was in important age-old questions such as anti-Semitism and the fulfillment of biblical prophesy. They were occupied with concerns of guilt over the Holocaust.

As Palestinian Christians, some of us began to ask, "Why can't we also have a dialogue with Jewish theologians?" However, what was of interest to us was a completely different agenda. What about reconciliation and coexistence? What about justice? How could we engage in mutual dialogue by reading the Bible together?

Structures for dialogue had to be imposed from the outside. In fact, they began on European soil, not during an era of cooperation, but when things looked desperate during the first Intifada. The Jewish–Christian dialogue, surprisingly, was not a natural development. It had to be forced. It had to be developed with a lot of patience and forbearance.

First Trialogue: Sweden, 1990

The first gathering took place in 1990 in Sigtuna, Sweden—a trialogue at the Life and Peace Institute funded by the Church of Sweden.[2] There was every reason that we should have expected failure at this first venture of interfaith discussion. In fact, failure would have been much easier than success.

This occasion was long before any breakthrough in the peace process. It was still illegal for Israelis even to talk with the PLO, and many Palestinians were reluctant to recognize Israel's right to exist. Those of us who came as representatives of our respective faiths and as participants in trialogue were chosen by our constituencies.

The theme for the conference was "The Holy Land in the Monotheistic Faiths." Speakers from each faith presented papers, and heated discussions followed. We did not avoid accusations at this first conference. "You Jews, don't you realize that you have treated us this way?" "You Muslims, you have done this." And so it went. There was a necessary outpouring of anger, fueled by years of misunderstanding and the misuse of religion due to separation. For those of us sitting there, this seemed like such a futile idea. How was it possible to break the impasse?

Looking around the room, I was somewhat timid. What might I have to offer that could change these deeply embedded feelings of mistrust and suspicion? Still, something moved me to open my mouth. I spoke not of anger but of fear.

"My son is only seven years old. He lives in constant terror that IDF patrols will hurt him. Last month when a curfew was imposed upon Ramallah, he was playing in the courtyard of our house, climbing on a wall. When he saw the military Jeep advance down the street, he was so afraid that he jumped down from the wall, nearly three meters down to the pavement, injuring his leg. Why? They likely would have ignored him, just a child. Yet he was afraid. I do not want my child to grow in hatred and fear. This is the way we live." I told my story, then sat quietly.

Immediately, an Israeli rabbi responded. "I have a three-year-old daughter," he said. "I am afraid she will pass through the Old City and be stabbed by Arabs."

There was a long silence. I consider it to be like the "silence" of Revelation 8:1. It seemed that we had found each other's humanity of suffering and pain. Yet the tone of the conference changed. We were no longer hurling accusations but expressing deep-seated fears. It was honest and frank communication. We had begun to talk, person to person.

Then came the question, "What can religion contribute in this situation?"

The Swedish conveners suggested that we write a common statement. The Jewish participants, however, wanted three separate statements. We argued about the statements. I stressed the importance of a single statement. Finally, we decided that each group would write down their ideas as a first step, and then, perhaps, we could come together to formulate a common statement.

The Muslims and Christians agreed that we would work together because of our same shared experience. Dr. Diab Ayyoush of Bethlehem University and I were assigned to produce a first draft. In thirty minutes we were finished. The other Muslims and Christians were satisfied with what we had written. So we all went outside to relax and to enjoy the outdoors. The Jews, however, continued for long hours and still had not reached agreement.

When we finally came back to the plenary session, there was bickering. Palestinians argued, "You Jews go first." Then someone from the

Jewish side stood up to propose that there should be two separate Jewish statements. Finally, the Palestinians agreed to read their statement, followed by the Jews. There were many striking commonalities. It seemed that we had made progress.

However, we began to dwell on differences. In the Muslim–Christian statement, we had written, "How can religion positively contribute to a just peace in the Middle East?"

Yes, this was good, the Israelis announced. But it was necessary to delete the word "just" as sounding too leftist. Other Israelis, however, expressed a feeling of guilt. They spoke as if they were ashamed that their government was the occupier against unarmed Palestinians. Still others argued that they were only defending themselves.

Some debated whether we should be involved in a dialogue or a trialogue. Some Israelis were more reluctant to speak with the Muslims than with Christians. Some Muslims wanted their views expressed separately from the Christians.

All this was a significant lesson in our own education, because we were confronting important issues for the first time.

Then, the news report came from Israel. The Jewish fundamentalist Kahane had been killed. Some Palestinians reacted rather bluntly: "One who uses force in his life, will by force be taken."

Jewish members expressed displeasure: "We disagree with Kahane, but killing cannot be accepted."

A lively discussion followed. We were faced with reality. The conference was not dealing only with the theoretical; it had life-and-death implications. We had many disagreements, but we took our task very seriously. In the end, we produced a good common statement.

The Beginning of Informal Discussions

We also started a long-term process of discussion. We agreed to continue the trialogue back home in Israel and Palestine, under two conditions. First, discussions should be local. This should not be something manipulated by European and American religious leaders. Second, we should be discrete. The more open we were at this stage, the more danger there was of misunderstanding by uninformed parties and of misinterpretation by those with political motivation.

We also initiated our efforts at social interaction. Through our time together in Sweden, we had broken down barriers, and we had begun friendships.

We continued to meet on a regular basis. We discovered how important this was a year later during the Gulf War. At a meeting at Hebrew Union College, questions and accusations were raised. "Why are Palestinians standing on rooftops cheering when Scud missiles are launched against Israel?"

This was a very difficult question for those of us who had begun the dialogue process. We began to talk more about the years of occupation and the pent-up anger of the Palestinian people. Many of our rabbi friends agreed. "We need to speak out more strongly concerning an end to occupation."

In 1993, when Rabin and Arafat shook hands on the White House lawn, these same rabbis telephoned to congratulate us on the major progress that had taken place.

Peace is *metanoia,* a change of mind. It is not practical, as the Bible says, to sew a new patch on an old cloak (Mark 2:21). A whole new fabric must be woven. We have seen that we can learn from our children. Society and families teach prejudice and stigmatization. That's why peace education must start from childhood. I was invited to give a talk at an Orthodox synagogue in the West Jerusalem neighborhood of Talpiot. Afterward, a sixty-year-old Jewish man came up to tell me that I was the first Palestinian Christian he had ever met.

The problem is demonization of the other. We react out of fear, and we dehumanize each other, because we simply do not know each other. I have learned that I do not really know much about Jewish customs, and I know that my ways are unfamiliar to Jews. We live separate lives and ignore each other. As religious leaders, we came to realize the need for more interaction, for a large seder to gather seventy or eighty people, for more public communications.

Second Trialogue: Switzerland, 1993

We made a lot of progress following our 1990 international trialogue in Sweden. It seemed, however, that we had reached a point where we needed another push. Through the initiative of the Lutheran World Federation's standing Committee on Human Rights and International Affairs, a second international trialogue was sponsored by the World Council of Churches in consultation with the Vatican.[3]

This time the colloquium was held in the small town of Glion in Switzerland from May 2 to 6, 1993. It was decided to keep the gathering small, with an equal number of participants from each group: ten Muslims, ten Jews, and ten Christians. The tone was different from that of the Swedish conference, because the Madrid Agreement on Principles had been signed, and the momentum was moving in the direction of a peaceful solution.

The gathering's theme was the spiritual significance of Jerusalem for Jews, Christians, and Muslims. Even though we had made an important beginning, it was clear that there was much work to be done. Following paper presentations, a number of the Jewish participants said, "We were simply unaware of this history. We had no idea why there were Christians in Jerusalem."

A Muslim from Hebron, Abu Malik, was asked to explain the expression "*Jihad* for Jerusalem." I was placed in the position of translator. This turned awkward for me, because he used words about fighting. At first, I tried to phrase things carefully in English so that it would not sound so offensive.

Abu Malik then began to get irritated and addressed me in front of the entire group in English, as best he could. "Yes, I want to tell them that if negotiations do not succeed, then war will succeed."

A number of Muslims interrupted to say that they disagreed with this viewpoint. They did not even want him to be allowed to continue. Others said that all views must be expressed. We all finally agreed that in a dialogue we need to discuss real issues, not surface issues.

We had reached a new level in the discussions. It was not enough to speak of the Christian view or the Jewish view or the Muslim view. There were multiple views in each tradition. We now faced the dilemma of discerning the various nuances of positions. In addition we began to address concerns about fundamentalist and fanatical groups who would not even participate in such discussions.

Although we had come a long way since the first trialogue in Sweden, it became more apparent that we had a long way to go.

Third Trialogue: Thessaloniki, 1997

The third trialogue took place in Thessaloniki, Greece, in 1997. This gathering was expanded by the presence of a large number of international participants. They included, for example, Rabbi James Rudin of the American Jewish Committee, rabbis from the United States and Europe, Muslims from around the world, and representatives from the World Council of Churches. It was apparent that Jerusalem plays a special role for the worldwide community of all three religions. We realized that we could not ignore or underestimate that, but, at the same time, that this phenomenon should not be overestimated.

When I arrived in Thessaloniki in late afternoon on the day before the conference, I was informed that one of the main speakers was unable to come. "Munib, you are the best-qualified person to address the topic, 'Living in Peace in Jerusalem,'" I was told. "You have to prepare a speech."

"Scheduled for what time?" I asked.

"Nine o'clock tomorrow morning," they responded.

It was impossible, I thought to myself. I am tired from traveling. I have no background papers with me. I will be facing many people I have never met before. What will I write? I stayed up most of the night and was very tired when the time came for the opening paper. It was clearly a matter of adrenaline keeping my body going.

I was assigned to talk about living in Jerusalem. How does one live in peace? I began simply by saying that living in peace is an art, an extraordinary art.

When one looks at the one-square-kilometer area known as the Old City, there are thirteen church leaders, and one mufti and in West Jerusalem there are two chief rabbis, one Sephardic and one Ashkenazi. In the Old City there is a Christian Quarter, an Armenian Quarter, a Muslim Quarter, and a Jewish Quarter. Life is rather complicated in the Old City. For the outsider, so much seems trivial. Yet for the person who has grown up there, living side by side with people of varying religious and ethnic backgrounds, one develops an understanding. It is an art. The key is getting to know both commonalities and differences. Through respecting the other, one learns to live in peace.

I'm not sure how brilliant my words were or whether I said anything really new or groundbreaking. However, my speech triggered an interesting discussion.

One Jewish participant raised the following question: "Why can I not pray on the Temple Mount?" No one, of course, foresaw how that question would play out several years later in triggering the al-Aqsa Intifada, when Ariel Sharon made an appearance at this sacred site to pray. Others, including a group called "The Temple Mount Faithful," want to make regular visits and to lay a cornerstone for a third Jewish temple. For outsiders, the question is real and pertinent.

The reaction of the Muslim participants demonstrated that it is a very emotional issue. "No, it is impossible. This is a Muslim area." The question should not even be held open for debate.

So there was an impasse. The hall was quiet. Since my presentation had sparked this discussion, the moderator turned to me. "Munib," he asked, "how can we live in Jerusalem in peace with rival claims to the one place some call the *Haram al-Sharif* and others call the Temple Mount?"

I sat quietly for a moment. What might I have to say to contribute to solving this age-old problem? Finally, I decided that I could only speak from my own experience.

"I am a Christian and a Lutheran," I began. "There is nothing more important to my faith than our teaching about the death of Jesus which saves me from my sins. Everything rests on this."

Many people began to wonder what this had to do with the controversy over the *Haram al-Sharif*/Temple Mount. But I kept going.

"The place for this core event of salvation is only one hundred meters or so from my own Lutheran Church of the Redeemer in the Old City. This is the Golgotha hill now contained inside the Church of the Holy Sepulchre. This Christian shrine is very dear to me. I often visit there. I take visitors there to show them. Yet, what would happen if I began to lead them in a hymn? What would happen if I led them in a prayer and began to shout 'Glory hallelujah'? We all know what would happen. A major controversy would break out among the churches of Jerusalem."

From the smiles on the participants' faces, it was clear that they understood. We Christians have plenty of stories about disputes over jurisdiction and practices within the Church of the Holy Sepulchre. Such disputes may seem very trivial to outsiders, yet to us from the Old City, they are very real. Through my story, I had turned their attention from a Muslim–Jewish dispute to one among Christians. Was I going to lay my claim to a piece of the Holy Sepulchre? No, of course not.

I continued, "I wouldn't even think of leading a prayer in the Church of the Holy Sepulchre. Christians in Jerusalem understand that prayers in the Church of the Holy Sepulchre are restricted to six of the thirteen churches. The *Status Quo* agreement established under the Ottoman Empire in 1852 helped set the parameters by which we Christians operate in Jerusalem. I wouldn't think of disputing that. This is what I mean when I say that living in Jerusalem is an art. For outsiders, it may sound trivial. Yet growing up in the shadow of the Church of the Holy Sepulchre, I have an appreciation and a respect for such historic agreements. I honor them and I live with my fellow Christians in peace."

What complicates the matter is that Jerusalem has been changing. More and more outsiders make pilgrimages to Jerusalem and do not understand this art of living together. More and more outsiders are moving in on a permanent basis, whether we like it or not. How does this affect our life together?

Some may also look at my approach to praying in the Holy Sepulchre as self-restraint. Should the Muslims also follow this policy and yield on the *Haram al-Sharif*/Temple Mount?

In this case, I would say no. I told the group, "The art of living in Jerusalem involves understanding the other. To the person raising this question, I would say, 'You need to understand Muslims. You need to learn about Islam.' Too many outsiders don't bother to do that."

I went on, "I have to speak for my Muslim neighbors. You may understand me as a Christian and have respect for me. Yet, as a Christian, I must ask you to try to understand the Muslim point of view. What has been their experience? To them, outsiders have come and have taken control. We all are selfish by nature. That's why we need restraints. Whatever we think about that site with respect to our history, this *Haram al-Sharif* has been for the Muslims a holy place for the past thirteen hundred years. We need to recognize this and to respect this. Secondly, there is the fear that you as Jews will first come to pray, and then you'll claim it. This fear is that you as Jews will first come to pray, and then you'll claim it. That is the experience from Hebron. First, Jews came to pray at Abraham's tomb. Then, we had the Goldstein massacre of Muslims there. Now, Muslims must go through Israeli control to pray in their own mosque. That is the experience. That is why I oppose any Jew praying at the *Haram al-Sharif*/Temple Mount."

I felt that I had contributed to a better understanding concerning the concept of sharing Jerusalem. I had not brought new ideas but the wisdom of having lived all my life in Jerusalem. I was sharing from my own experience how I have sought to live in peace with my neighbor.

There were many other excellent papers. Participants continued to wrestle with important issues. In the process, we continued to grow in our understanding of each other.

As with the previous conferences, the most difficult phase came when we began to write our final statement. Two major issues made this difficult.

First, there was a split between the international participants and those of us who lived in Jerusalem. This was especially the case among the Jewish participants. Yet, those of us who lived together—and who had now been engaged in dialogue for seven years—asserted our views to shape the statement. In the end, the American Jewish participants would not sign.

Second, a controversy developed over language in one particular section. Jewish participants had written that "Using religion to justify violence is unacceptable." Muslim participants became upset because they felt that the statement was specifically aimed at them. The Jewish participants, however, would not budge. The statement must be included or they would not sign. We had a deadlock.

It took a while. Patiently, we discussed the issue and finally came up with an acceptable change in wording, "No religion accepts violence." This way, the Jewish participants were able to emphasize this important aspect of living in peace, and yet it spoke of all of us as equals. The Muslims agreed to sign. The Jewish participants from Jerusalem agreed to sign.

In a sense, the conference itself had been a microcosm of what it means to live in peace with each other. This came about, of course, from long hours of listening to each other's positions and from our careful negotiations over our joint statement. It also benefited from the experience of our life together in informal settings.

Thessaloniki has its own religious history. It had once been home to a large Jewish population, and it had experienced Nazi occupation. Several rabbi colleagues from Jerusalem invited me and a Muslim friend to visit a local synagogue with them, where we were enriched by the experience. Then, they took us to a cemetery for Holocaust victims. It moved us to see how this experience affected them as Jews. This was all part of the process of growing closer together. Sometimes, we learn to live together first outside our own places. Then we return to Jerusalem with a better understanding of living together in peace.

This was the last of a series of international trialogues. They came about because of the impetus of outside groups. Unfortunately, no one saw fit to sponsor another such conference on European soil.

Secret Informal Trialogues: Jerusalem

We did have the opportunity for continued discussions in Jerusalem. Over a period of about a year beginning in 1998, the Norwegian Lutheran Church funded a series of five trialogues. These sessions differed from the international meetings in significant ways. First, they included a small number of leaders in the Muslim, Jewish, and Christian communities, so the meetings carried more of an aura of authority. Second, they were for much shorter periods. Third, they provided no opportunity for informal group building. The sessions were all held under a veil of secrecy at the Palestinian Academic Society for the Study of International Affairs (PASSIA) in East Jerusalem.

The first meeting took place during Ramadan in 1998. The topic naturally surfaced about the closures that prevented West Bank residents from coming to Jerusalem for Friday prayers.

"They can't?" exclaimed the Jewish rabbis, incredulous about the actual situation on the ground. The rest of us had assumed that Israelis understood the difficulties resulting from roadblocks and closures. This provided the perfect opportunity to discuss the realities of religious practice under military rule.

At the next meeting, the chief rabbi commented, "Have you noticed anything different?"

"The border patrol is allowing more worshipers through to Jerusalem," we chimed in unison. At first, there was a natural feeling of appreciation. The rabbis had noticed a practice that was not acceptable and, to their credit, they acted on it. Yet, what did this really mean? We needed to be careful that our meetings were not perceived as negotiating sessions where a weaker group (Christians and Muslims) sought special privileges from the powerful group (Jews). This was an issue of mere human rights and religious freedom, not a political bargaining session.

After this meeting, an Israeli reporter who had followed one of the rabbis confronted him outside. "What is going on? Are you following some separate track in political negotiations?"

Fortunately, the two Norwegians who were always present (one a church official, the other a government representative) intervened to protect the rabbi.

In February 1999, the last meeting in this series of discussions was held. The talks broke down over a conflict.

The topic was the role of the Holy Places. Israeli Rabbi Sirat, chief rabbi of France, began by telling a midrash. "There once was a stable where a horse was kept. One day when the horse went outside, an ox came and took his place. Later, the horse returned. What should be done? The stable is too small for both to live together. The only solution is that the ox must leave to make room for the horse."

Immediately, various participants began to speak up wondering what this was supposed to mean.

"It's just a midrash," responded Rabbi Sirat. "I didn't intend to say anything. I just thought it was interesting."

However, the flare-up demonstrates how insensitivity over words and symbols can be destructive to serious religious dialogue.

The Muslims asked, "Do you mean that we Muslims should leave the *Haram al-Sharif* so that you can rebuild your temple?"

The Christians asked, "Do you mean that we Palestinians must leave Jerusalem? the country?"

Rabbi Michael Melchior intervened: "Why are you attacking Rabbi Sirat? You are all making too much of this simple midrash."

Unfortunately, the die had been cast. "Is this the real face that you have been hiding throughout our discussions? Does not this show that we are unwanted?"

Everyone was boiling.

As the date of the next scheduled meeting approached, various participants began to offer excuses. The Norwegian mediators tried to salvage the discussions. Finally, the mufti of Jerusalem made a formal announcement: "There will be no dialogue until the peace treaty is signed."

At the time, the Wye Conference had been announced, and many expected fairly rapid progress toward a full peace treaty. Then, we would be back in discussions. However, that did not happen. The Muslims had taken a stand that they would not revoke, saying that they would not meet. The Jews tried to encourage the Christians to keep the talks going, but we decided that we could not continue talks on this level without Muslim participation.

Talks like this are precarious, sometimes like trying to walk on a tightrope. Now, we had stumbled and could not get our balance. All momentum was lost, and we haven't met since that February 1999 meeting.

This is a reminder that it is often much easier to fail than to succeed.

Papal Jubilee Year Pilgrimage

The breakdown of formal discussions set the backdrop for the papal Jubilee visit in March 2000. News coverage of his visit centered on John Paul's own yearning to visit the Holy Places, his dramatic mea culpa for Christian mistakes against Judaism, and his stand in solidarity with Palestinian Christians. He was also concerned to demonstrate the importance of interreligious dialogue in this city holy to the three monotheistic faiths.

The interfaith meeting took place on a Tuesday evening at the Notre Dame Center just outside the Old City. The gathering was expected to be a public demonstration of cooperation for the world. Children's choirs lined the stage to entertain the guests. The pope was seated in a prominent position. The planned climax for the evening was to be a round of handshaking among the participants and planting an olive tree together.

Yet, the ground was not fertile for the desired outcome. It had not been well prepared nor had it been plowed. The two speakers were Rabbi Lau, the chief rabbi of Jerusalem, who had not participated in any of the previous interfaith discussions, and the deputy chief judge of the Islam court, Sheik Tayseer Tamimi, who had publicly separated himself from formal discussions. There was no role for a Palestinian Christian voice. Rather, the pope himself would speak briefly on behalf of Christians.

Rabbi Lau was given the floor to speak first. Basically he gave a good speech, that is, until the end. At that point, he turned from religious dialogue to pure politics. "Jerusalem is Israel's united eternal capital," he announced to the crowd. "The pope's presence recognizes this fact."[4]

At that point Afif Safieh, the PLO representative to the Vatican, said out loud, "Not true. Not true. Here is the pope. Ask him."

Lau, however, went to shake hands as if there were nothing extraordinary about his words.

It was now the turn of Tamimi. Standing at the podium, he made an obvious display of putting away his prepared text. Instead, he began to address the pope. "I welcome you, Pope John Paul," he said in Arabic, "as guest of the state of Palestine in our eternal capital of Jerusalem, *al-Quds al Sharif.*"

Again, the Palestinian crowd reacted with cheers. Then Tamimi continued to speak in Arabic about the many of the issues facing the Palestinians: confiscation of Jerusalem IDs, closures, checkpoints, and so on. Finishing his ad-lib remarks, he, too, shook hands and sat down.

Throughout his trip, the pope's frail condition received a lot of attention. In contrast to the somewhat flamboyant styles of the first two speakers, the pontiff slowly walked to the podium and seemed to struggle even to project his words. He made a long speech about dialogue among the three religions. Here he made a reference to 1 John 4:20: "If you say you love God and hate your brother, you are a liar."

At this, Tamimi left the stage. Apparently, he had excused himself to the pope in order to say evening prayers. However, it was obvious to all that the proposed planting of an olive tree had gone by the wayside. Was this session a fiasco, as the *Jerusalem Post* suggested? No, it was a bitter reality. There can be no true dialogue without paying attention to reality.

The decade of the 1990s in many ways provided a lot of promise for Jewish-Christian-Muslim trialogue. How sad that the new millennium began on such an ominous note. Much progress seemed to be lost, and discussions seemed to be at a standstill. It seemed to be a foreshadowing of more difficult days to come.

Interreligious Coordinating Council in Israel

When the al-Aqsa Intifada began in late September 2000, Rabbi Ron Kronish of the Interreligious Coordinating Council in Israel (ICCI) called to ask if we might gather as religious leaders. Since much of the early activity had centered on the Mount of Olives, he suggested that we hold a joint prayer service at Augusta Victoria Hospital. The situation at Augusta Victoria had been politicized, however, by West Jerusalem's Mayor Olmert, so we chose rather to meet at the Apostolic Delegate. Because of Muslim views, we decided against the idea of a common prayer. The situation demanded that we at least produce a common statement.

"I think it is important for me to come to you," said Rabbi Kronish. "Yet, I do have real concerns for my own safety."

I assured him that his security was with me. This is what a decade of dialogue had accomplished. Our personal relationships had been enhanced. We lived together in an attitude of trust. So together, we drove to the meeting on the Mount of Olives. Together, we hammered out a common statement. When it was presented to the board members of ICCI—Muslims, Jews, and Christians—it met unanimous approval.

Through the influence of the ICCI, the following statement was published in *Ha'aretz* on October 13, 2000.

An Emergency Appeal to Religious and Political Leaders

As men and women of faith, affiliated with the three mono-theistic religions in Israel—Judaism, Christianity, and Islam—we address this appeal to religious and political leaders on both sides of the conflict because we are urgently concerned about the escalating spiral of violence in Israel and Palestine, with a growing number of injured and dead.

First, we appeal to religious leaders in the Jewish, Christian, and Muslim communities in this land at all levels. We ask them to raise their voices for sanity and for peace. We appeal to them to speak prophetically and courageously to their followers:

- To inculcate the values of truth, justice, and love of one's fellow human being, based on the principle "Love your neighbor as yourself" and the practice of reconciliation;
- To condemn, in no uncertain terms, the practice of provocative rhetoric, vengeance and violence, by individuals and groups, both against human beings and the holy sites of all religious groups;
- To reinforce the basic value that every human being is created in the image of God so that all human beings have a right to life;
- To express sympathy and empathy for the loss of life on both sides of the conflict, by expressing heartfelt condolences to both Palestinian and Israeli families who have lost loved ones in the tragic fighting that has already occurred, and to extend good wishes for speedy recoveries for all the injured in the hospitals who are struggling for their lives;

- To ensure that territorial disagreements should not be transformed into religious wars.

Second, we appeal to the political leaders — on both sides of the conflict — to return to the path of peace, through the peace process. We remind them that achieving peace will not merely be a victory for the political leaders, but also for the peoples in the region who strive to live in dignity and with security. To achieve peace, it will be necessary for each side to stop blaming each other and to abide by agreements already reached. Rather, it is essential to reengage in confidence-building measures that enable the development of cooperation and trust. The peace process begins with the basic idea of respect for the life of each and every member of the two peoples. Rather than continuing to engage in violence and counterviolence, it is urgent for political leaders on both sides to open their minds and hearts to the human, political, religious and civil rights and aspirations of the other as well as to those of their own people.

The Alexandria Agreement

Over a year passed while the whole peace process unraveled before our eyes. In January 2002, however, there was a resurgence of interest in dialogue at the encouragement of the Archbishop of Canterbury, George Carey. Meeting in Alexandria, Egypt, high-ranking rabbis, church leaders, and imams came together for discussions and signed an agreement to dedicate ourselves to the continuation of dialogue, to work for justice and peace, to strive for the ending of occupation and the spiral of violence. This included specific reference to the Mitchell Report and the Tenet Plan which had been put forth by the United States.

The Alexandria agreement reached a second phase through an October 2002 conference at Lambeth Palace in London. Eight Jewish rabbis, eights heads of churches, and eight imams came together again to wrestle with these issues at a time when the political process for peace had seemingly reached rock bottom. The Israeli army had reoccupied every Palestinian city. The Palestinian President Yasser Arafat had been besieged and rendered powerless in his bombed out compound in Ramallah. Suicide bombings continued. Suffering was all around as the death toll on both sides continued to rise.

Yet from a theological perspective we had to hold out a word of hope. We had to assure the world that the process of dialogue itself was important.

Still, there were no easy answers. The Palestinian Christian and Muslim representatives emphasized in the talks that the end of occupation was the key to ending violence. The Jewish representatives countered that an end of violence must precede an end to occupation. For some, such an impasse would be reason to throw up our hands in resignation. For others, this was all the more reason that dialogue must continue.

Do we have a choice? For myself, this is my calling as the Lutheran Bishop of Jerusalem. We have been called as witnesses of peace from Jerusalem to the ends of the earth.

Notes

Chapter 1

1. Three excellent sources for this history are Donald E. Wagner, *Dying in the Land of Promise: Palestine and Palestinian Christianity from Pentecost to 2000* (London: Melisende, 2001); Karen Armstrong, *Jerusalem: One City, Three Faiths* (New York: Ballantine, 1996); Kenneth Cragg, *The Arab Christian: A History in the Middle East* (Louisville, Ky.: Westminster John Knox, 1991).

2. Eusebius, *Ecclesiastical History* 2.23.18, quoting Hegesippus, a second-century Christian writer living in Palestine. Note the interest in the newly discovered ossuary of James in André Lemaire, "Burial Box of James the Brother of Jesus," *Biblical Archaeology Review* 28:6 (November–December 2002): 24–33.

3. Eusebius, *Ecclesiastical History* 4.5.

4. Jerome Murphy-O'Connor, "Pre-Constantinian Christian Jerusalem," in *The Christian Heritage in the Holy Land*, ed. Anthony O'Mahony, Göran Gunner, and Kevork Hintlian (London: Scorpion Cavendish, 1995), 16–17.

5. Eusebius, *Ecclesiastical History* 6.11.

6. Mitri Raheb and Fred Strickert, *Bethlehem 2000: Past and Present* (Heidelberg: Palmyra, 1998), 77–87; Derwas J. Chitty, *The Desert a City: An Introduction to the Study of Egyptian and Palestinian Monasticism under the Christian Empire* (Oxford: Blackwell, 1966). See also Yoram Tsafrir, *Ancient Churches Revealed* (Jerusalem: Israel Exploration Society, 1993).

7. Cragg, *The Arab Christian*, 42–43.

8. Ibid., 52–55; John C. Lamoreaux, "Early Eastern Christian Responses to Islam," in *Medieval Christian Perceptions of Islam*, ed. John Victor Tolan (New York: Routledge, 2000), 3–32.

9. Ibid., 56–59.

10. Muqaddas, *Description of Syria*, 37, quoted by Armstrong, *Jerusalem*, 257.

11. Mitri Raheb, *I Am a Palestinian Christian*, trans. Ruth C. L. Gritsch (Minneapolis: Fortress Press, 1995), 9.

12. Armstrong, *Jerusalem*, 258–62.

13. Cragg, *The Arab Christian*, 71–94.

14. Sidney H. Griffith, *Arabic Christianity in the Monasteries of Ninth-Century Palestine* (Brookfield, Vt.: Variorum, 1992).

15. Cragg, *The Arab Christian*, 62–66.

16. Armstrong, *Jerusalem*, 271–94.

17. Ibid., 284.

18. Wagner, *Dying*, 69–71.

19. Armstrong, *Jerusalem*, 325.

20. Ibid., 347.

21. Ibid., 347–49.

22. Mitri Raheb, *Das reformatorische Erbe unter den Palästinensern: zur Entstehung der Evangelisch-Lutherischen Kirche in Jordanien* (Gütersloh: Gütersloher Verlagshaus, 1990).

23. Cragg, *The Arab Christian*, 282–85.

24. Adnan Musallam, "The Formative Stages of Palestinian Emigration to the Americas... until the Eve of the 1948 Catastrophe," *Al-Liqa' Journal* 2 (December 1992): 17–41, especially 18; Bernard Sabella, "The Emigration of Christian Arabs: Dimensions and Causes of the Phenomenon," in *Christian Communities in the Arab Middle East: The Challenge of the Future*, ed. Andrea Pacini (Oxford: Clarendon, 1998), 131.

25. Figures derived from Naim Stifan Ateek, *Justice, and Only Justice: A Palestinian Theology of Liberation* (Maryknoll, N.Y.: Orbis, 1989), 53, and Wagner, *Dying*, 81.

26. Chart is based on a chart in Armstrong, *Jerusalem*, 352, with additions from Armstrong, *Jerusalem*, 324–25, 347 and Wagner, *Dying*, 150, 209.

27. Cragg, *The Arab Christian*, 265.

28. Ibid., 161–66.

29. Wagner, *Dying*, especially 129–55.

30. Figures based on maps prepared by the United Nations as printed in Walid Khalidi, ed., *All That Remains: The Palestinian Villages Occupied and Depopulated by Israel in 1948* (Washington, D.C.: Institute for Palestine Studies), and Wagner, *Dying*, 191–92, 227.

31. Ilan Pappe, *The Making of the Arab-Israeli Conflict: 1947–51* (New York: St. Martin's, 1994); Benny Morris, *Righteous Victims: A History of the Zionist-Arab Conflict, 1881–1999* (New York: Knopf, 1999).

32. For the story of the loss of the Christian village of Bir'im, see Elias Chacour with David Hazard, *Blood Brothers* (Grand Rapids, Mich.: Chosen, 2003).

33. For more on the Bethlehem congregations, see Raheb, *I Am a Palestinian Christian,* and the review of this book by Fred Strickert in *Currents in Theology and Mission* (February 1998): 46–52. Also Raheb and Strickert, *Bethlehem 2000.*

34. *Annual Report 1999:* ELCJ (Jerusalem).

Chapter 2

1. Walid Khalidi, ed., *All That Remains: The Palestinian Villages Occupied and Depopulated by Israel in 1948* (Washington, D.C.: Institute for Palestine Studies, 1992), 71–78.

2. See Walid Khalidi, *Before Their Diaspora: A Photographic History of the Palestinians 1876–1948* (Washington, D.C.: Institute for Palestinian Studies 1991), 305–45.

3. Elias Chacour with David Hazard, *Blood Brothers* (Grand Rapids, Mich.: Chosen Books, 2003).

4. Khalidi, *All That Remains,* 460–61.

5. Ibid., 5.

6. Sydney Gruson, "Israel Claims Route of Arabs in the North," *New York Times,* November 1, 1949, 1, 3. The cost to the Israelis was only nine dead in the campaign, which added 250 square miles to Israel.

7. As recently as 1997, former residents of Bir'im have presented formal appeals to the Israeli government. After seven delays, the Israeli Security Cabinet ruled once again in October 2001 against the return of the residents of Bir'im. Aluf Benn, "Cabinet Rejects Biram and Ikrit Villagers' Plea to Return," *Ha'aretz,* October, 10 2001.

Chapter 3

1. *Boston Globe* reporter Charles M. Sennott recounts his confusion in *The Body and the Blood: The Holy Land's Christians at the Turn of the New Millennium: A Reporter's Journey* (New York: Public Affairs, 2001), 399.

2. H. Strathmann, "*martys,*" in *Theological Dictionary of the New Testament,* vol. 4, ed. Gerhard Kittel (Grand Rapids, Mich.: Eerdmans, 1967), 494.

3. Ibid., 476.

4. Munib A. Younan, "Election in Deutero-Isaiah" (thesis for the degree of Master of Theology presented to the Faculty of Theology, University of Helsinki, Finland, 1976).

5. The Septuagint (Greek) translation uses several forms of *martys* here.

6. Eusebius, *Ecclesiastical History* 4.15. Translation as used in *Eerdman's Handbook to the History of Christianity,* ed. Tim Dowley (Herts, England: Lion, 1977), 81. Or quoted in Frederich Schumacher, *For All the Saints* (New York: American Lutheran Publicity Bureau, 1995), 60–61.

7. Thomas à Kempis, *Of the Imitation of Christ* (London: Oxford Univ. Press, 1961), 4.

Chapter 4

1. A form of this chapter was published as "The Land from a Christian Perspective," *Al-Liqa' Journal* (June/December 1997): 57–70.

2. Colin Chapman, *Whose Promised Land?* (Oxford: Lion, 1992). More recently, Chapman has addressed the issue in "Ten Questions for a Theology of the Land," in *The Land of Promise: Biblical, Theological, and Contemporary Perspectives,* ed. Philip Johnston and Peter Walker (Downers Grove, Ill.: Intervarsity, 2000), 172–87.

3. Michel Sabbah, "Reading the Bible Today in the Land of the Bible," *Al-Liqa' Journal* (November 1993): 49–60, especially 49.

4. Naim Stifan Ateek, *Justice, and Only Justice: A Palestinian Theology of Liberation* (Maryknoll, N.Y.: Orbis, 1989), 86–89. See also James Limburg, *The Prophets and the Powerless* (Atlanta: John Knox, 1977).

5. Walter Brueggemann, *The Land: Place as Gift, Promise, and Challenges in Biblical Faith,* 2d ed. (Minneapolis: Fortress Press, 2002), 2.

6. Ibid., 10.

7. Ibid., 160–63.

8. W. D. Davies: *The Gospel and the Land: Early Christianity and Jewish Territorial Doctrine* (Berkeley: Univ. of California Press, 1974), 396–404; Brueggemann, *The Land,* 160.

9. Brueggemann, *The Land,* 165.

10. Ibid., 169.

11. Ibid., xv.

12. Rafiq Khoury, *The Significance of Jerusalem for Jews Christians and Muslims* (Geneva: World Council of Churches).

13. Karen Armstrong, *Jerusalem: One City, Three Faiths* (New York: Ballantine, 1996), 179–90. See also Robert L. Wilken, *The Land Called Holy: Palestine in Christian History and Thought* (New Haven: Yale Univ. Press, 1992), 101–25.

14. Athanasius, *Festal Letters* 3.5; 6.12; 19.8.

15. Cyril of Jerusalem, *Catechetical Lectures* 14.23.

16. Peter Walker, *Jerusalem: Past and Present in the Purposes of God,* (Cambridge: Cambridge Univ. Press, 1992), 79–97. See also Armstrong, *Jerusalem,* 190–91.

17. Jerome, *Letter to Marcella*, 386.

18. Naim Ateek, "Biblical Perspectives on the Land," in *Faith and the Intifada: Palestinian Christian Voices*, ed. Naim Ateek, Marc H. Ellis, and Rosemary Radford Ruether (Maryknoll, N.Y.: Orbis, 1992), 108–13, especially 111–12.

19. Sabbah, "Reading the Bible Today in the Land of the Bible," 58.

20. Pope Paul VI in *Animo* (March 25, 1974), quoted in George Emile Irani, *The Papacy and the Middle East: The Role of the Holy See in the Arab-Israeli Conflict, 1962–1984* (Notre Dame, Ind.: Univ. of Notre Dame Press, 1986), 84.

Chapter 5

1. Karl Barth, *Church Dogmatics*, vol. 2 (Edinburgh: T & T Clark, 1957), 386. See also James Limburg, *The Prophets and the Powerless* (Atlanta: John Knox, 1977).

2. The theme of justice in the Palestinian context is developed more fully in Naim Stifan Ateek, *Justice, and Only Justice: A Palestinian Theology of Liberation* (Maryknoll, N.Y.: Orbis, 1989).

3. "Statement Issued by the Heads of the Christian Communities in Jerusalem," January 22, 1988, reprinted in full in Mitri Raheb, *I Am a Palestinian Christian* (Minneapolis: Fortress Press, 1995), 123–24.

4. Sami Hadawi, *Palestinian Rights and Losses in 1948* (Amman, Jordan: Saqi, 1988), 136.

5. "Significance of Jerusalem for Christians: Memorandum of the Patriarchs and Heads of the Christian Communities in Jerusalem, November 14, 1994," in *Jerusalem, What Makes for Peace!*, ed. Naim Ateek, Cedar Duaybis, and Marla Schrader (London: Melisende, 1997), 236–41.

Chapter 6

1. Martin Luther King Jr., *Strength to Love* (New York: Harper & Row, 1963), 37.

2. UNRWA Press Release (United Nations Relief and Works Agency), December 10, 2002, listed on http://www.un.org/unrwa/.

3. *The Kairos Document—Challenge to the Church: A Theological Comment on the Political Crisis in South Africa* (Grand Rapids, Mich.: Eerdmans, 1985), 31–32. I credit Naim Ateek for calling this document to my attention in his *Justice, and Only Justice: A Palestinian Theology of Liberation* (Maryknoll, N.Y.: Orbis, 1989), 137.

4. Ami Ayalon was head of Shin Bet, the Israeli domestic security agency, from February 1996 to May 2000 under Prime Ministers Netanyahu

and Barak. He speaks further on this matter in Alain Cypel, "Interview with Ami Ayalon," *Le Monde,* December 22, 2001.

5. "Palestinian Man's Organs Save Israelis," Associated Press, June 5, 2001.

6. "Palestinian Heart Saves Life of Dying Israeli," Reuters, June 5, 2001.

7. One of the ironies is that many of the British who took the lead in supporting Zionism and the return of Jews to Palestine, such as Lord Balfour and David Lloyd George, were motivated by a dispensationalist view of Christianity that saw the Jews as having a divine right to the land. Donald E. Wagner, *Dying in the Land of Promise: Palestine and Palestinian Christianity from Pentecost to 2000* (London: Melisende, 2001), 99–100.

8. Donald E. Wagner, "Evangelicals and Israel: Theological Roots of a Political Alliance," *Christian Century* 115:30 (November 2, 1998): 1020–26.

9. Charles A. Kimball, "Roots of Rancor: Examining Islamic Militancy," *Christian Century* 118:29 (October 24–31, 2001): 18–23.

10. Cardinal Francis Arinze, "Christian-Muslim Relations at the Threshold of the Third Millennium," lecture during visit to Jerusalem at Notre Dame Center sponsored by the Apostolic Delegate in Jerusalem, February 28, 2001.

11. Riah Abu El-Assal, *Caught in Between: The Story of an Arab Palestinian Christian Israeli* (London: SPCK, 1999).

12. Kenneth L. Woodward, "How Should We Think about Islam?" *Newsweek* (December 31, 2001): 102–4.

13. Proceedings: World Council of Churches: Multifaith Consultation on Religious Education, Bangkok, October 11–15, 2000.

Chapter 7

1. Speech by Nunit Peled-Elhanan to Women in Black vigil in Jerusalem on Friday, June 8, 2001 (translated by the author herself), distributed by Gila Svirsky of Women in Black.

Chapter 8

1. Angus Deming, "The New War on Terrorism," *Newsweek* (October 31, 1977), 48–56; "War without Boundaries," *Time* (October 31, 1977), 28–31; and "Terror and Triumph at Mogadishu," *Time* (October 31, 1977), 42–44.

Chapter 9

1. This chapter was first presented as part of a lecture series at Notre Dame Center in Jerusalem in the spring of 1998. A form of it was later published as "Prayer and Reconciliation in a Shared Land," in *Toward the Third*

Millennium: Trialogue in Jerusalem: Jews, Christians, and Muslims, ed. Ron Kronish (Jerusalem: Interreligious Coordinating Council in Israel, 1999), 13–17.

2. Walter Brueggemann, *The Creative Word: Canon as a Model for Biblical Education* (Philadelphia: Fortress Press, 1982), 20.

3. Hans Küng, "No World Peace without Religious Peace," in *Christianity and the World Religions: Paths to Dialogue with Islam, Hinduism, and Buddhism,* Hans Küng et al., trans. Peter Heinegg (Garden City, N.Y.: Doubleday, 1986), 440–41, quote from 443.

Chapter 11

1. Krister Stendahl, *Paul among Jews and Gentiles, and Other Essays* (Philadelphia: Fortress Press, 1976), 37.

2. Munib Younan, "The Holy Land in the Christian Tradition," in *The Holy Land in the Monotheistic Faiths: Conference Report,* ed. Roger Williamson (Uppsala: Life and Peace Institute, 1992), 38–50.

3. *The Spiritual Significance of Jerusalem for Jews, Christians, and Muslims: A Report on a Colloquium in Glion, Switzerland, 2–6 May, 1993,* ed. Hans Ueko (Geneva: World Council of Churches, 1993).

4. Gil Hoffman, "PA Religious Court Head Attacks Israel in Interfaith Session," *Jerusalem Post,* March 24, 2000, 3a.